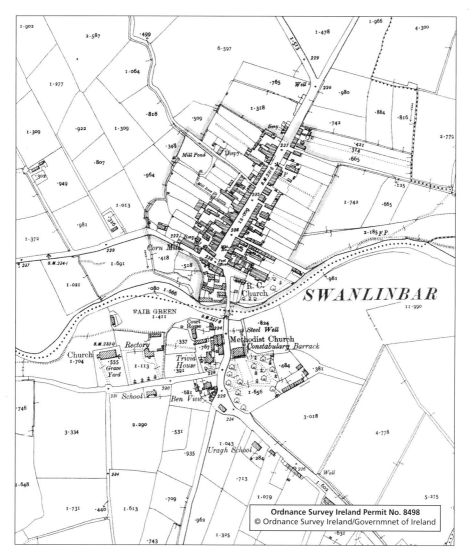

Ordnance Survey map of Swanlinbar, circa 1899.

JOE PRIOR

THAT'S THE WAY

'It takes a village to rear a child'
An old African saying

For my parents, Alice and Johnny Prior,
Aunty Kathleen, my sisters, Etta and Teresa
and all the people of Swad who reared me.

First published in 2008 by
Ben Aughlin Publications
22, The Park Drive,
Strandhill Road, Sligo
thepriors@eircom.net
t +353 (0)71 9161440/0876149135

ISBN: 978-0-9560575-0-1

Typeset and designed by Martin Corr at 8ball design

Text set in Anziano by Fountain

Printed and bound by Turner Print, Longford

Cover Images:

Background: Uragh scholars, 1950
Inset Photos: Right to left
Red Sunbeam Showband

Jimmy Whelan and John Devine
bringing home the bacon Swad style! Photo: Elsie (Howden) Abbott

Bathing Pool Bundoran

Back Cover Images:

Inset Photos: Right to left
Sonny Mac mending a bike outside his shop alongside the New Bridge while Mamie Reilly
maintains a watching brief! (1949)

Dan O' Rourke (Roscommon), President of the G.A.A., Comdt. John Joe O' Reilly (Cavan captain),
Sean T. O' Ceallaigh, President of Ireland, Dinny Lyne (Kerry captain), Bean Ui Ceallaigh and
Eamon de Valera, Taoiseach, at the Presidential reception for the Cavan and Kerry teams in Aras
an Uachtarain. Photo- Sr. Elizabeth O' Rourke, Sligo

Mullan Bridge. This bridge, situated at Mullan, one mile from Swanlinbar on the main Swanlinbar-
Enniskillen road, was blown up by the I.R.A. in 1961 during the final phase of the 'Operation
Harvest' campaign. Photo: Kelvin Boyes Photography

Photo of 1947 All Ireland Winning Cavan Team (p26) coutesy of Frank Burke

ACKNOWLEDGEMENTS

'That's the Way', which grew out of a persistent urge to focus on the village I left almost forty years ago and recreate the world I knew there as a child, would never have seen the light of day but for all who encouraged and helped me on my way.

I thank especially my wife, Margaret, and my four children, Fiona, Cara, Dearbhaile and John Paul. My older sisters, Etta and Teresa, verified the accuracy of my earliest recollections and shed light on my more shadowy memories. I thank the very helpful staff in Cavan, Sligo and Enniskillen libraries, Patrick Yeats, E.S.B. archives, Dublin, Dominic Kirwan and Savina Donohoe, Cavan County Museum, Ballyjamesduff, Prin Duignan, Manorhamilton, Pauline Leary of 'The Fermanagh Herald' and Johnny O'Hanlon, 'The Anglo Celt' for permission to use extracts from their files, Bill Mc Loughlin and D.C. Thomson and Co. Ltd. for permission to include images from the Beano, Alison Foley, Cantec, Sligo, Martin Corr at 8Ball Graphics and Turner Printing, Longford, for their professional work on layout and printing. I am also indebted to my friend and former teaching colleague, Pat Mc Loughlin, Bundoran for his proof reading and valued suggestions and Dermot Healy for his Foreword and general appraisal. Of course, I cannot forget those who contributed photos, gave generously of their time to fill in some background information or helped out in other ways: Mary Kenny, Essex, England, Anne and Noel Coffey, Belturbet, Frank Mc Govern, Ballintrillick, Co. Sligo, Sr. Elizabeth O'Rourke, Mercy, Sligo, Carrie Howden, Brackley, Bawnboy and Kathleen Plunkett, Bawnboy, Mary Gallagher (nee Mc Govern), Blacklion, Elsie Abbott (nee Howden), Florencecourt, Co. Fermanagh, Sharon Mc Namee and John Graham, Newbliss, Co. Monaghan, Michael Leydon, Sean Gilheaney, Ben Mc Hugh, Patsy Hughes (nee Woods), T.P. Prior, Andy Kelly and the late Frank Reilly, Swanlinbar, P.J. Dunne and Peadar Cassidy, Cavan, Joe Chapman, Bundoran and Kelvin Boyes, Press Eye Ltd, Belfast. Sean Gallagher and his good Belcoo wife, Mary, turned their house in Bundoran upside down to find that elusive photo of the Red Sunbeam showband and also drafted in their son, Johnny, to give me a helping hand

To one and all, a very sincere 'Thank you'.

Contents

The Tullydermot falls. These are situated 6km south-west of Swanlinbar on the southern slopes of the Cuilcagh mountains. They are well sign-posted, lie close to a lay-by and are easily accessible via the Mill Street exit from the village.

FOREWORD

'That's the Way is written by a gifted list-maker. Joe Prior at times enters the story of Swanlinbar personally, but mostly he is putting down on record the life of a small town from around the 50's, and he does so in both the scholarly and communal manner of the old Bards who remembered lost sensations for us all.

He knits the history of Swad- that took its name from Swift, Sanders, Darling and Barry- from the time when it was an iron centre to its period as a fashionable spa (until Viscount Enniskillen built a lodge in beautiful Bundoran, and the tourists moved to the Star of the Sea in sensible swim suits); and on to its days on the border as a centre of republicanism and football.

He turns the radio on to listen to All Irelands and in the door comes Micheal O'Hehir and John Joe O' Reilly, then Din Joe, and later on Jerry Lee Lewis with *Great Balls of Fire*, then the Royal Showband with *Kiss me Quick*. For years the village was a smuggling depot and the list of items smuggled across the border in the first 3 months of 1947 included - 8 coffins and 114,00 fishing hooks. He calls up all kinds of memories in impeccable lists; from Aspro and Vick and Sloans for Sciatica, Dolly Mixture and Gobstoppers to the Hail Holy Queen, Se Do Bheatha Bhaile, and Bheir Mi O. He notes the danger of accidentally sitting on a bed of pissmires how the barber would hoist him up on a plank placed across an armchair to cut his hair around the time he was learning:

> *Janey Mac, me shirt is black*
> *What will I do for Sunday?*
> *Go to bed and bury your head*
> *And don't get up till Monday.*

Sin lurks in the shadows, there were long piss competitions; locks went up on the gate leading to the hayshed to stop courting couples rolling in the hay when there was a dance in St. Mary's ; ESB lights went on with an official switch for 500 houses in 1953 in Swad and Templeport; The Beano and the Dandy and Bunty and Judy take to the floor ; and sometimes he hits the nail on the head when his memory brings back the simple joy of seeing a cow's apparent smile as she shook her head, swished her tail and chewed on a winter's night, or when he lets go with a great description of Enniskillen rail station.

He sets out a list of songs, football players, priests, superstitions and the terror of the repeated bombing of the Mullen custom hut up the road. He writes of the loss of a St. Pat's friend, who was shot dead. He itemizes what could be bought for a penny, and that included - a writing nib, a bar of toffee, an ice lolly, a pencil and fishing hook. His ear collects the guff perfectly- skid marks, Shank's mare, the poor bastes and the lock of onions, and election time when *" we come before you to stand behind you to tell you some   something we know nothing about"*.

Chickens arrive again from Elm Bank hatchery, and there's the rattle of bottles from Cavan Mineral Waters. And again Santa left part of his whiskers on the glass of port he'd drank on Christmas eve night. Joe Prior's nose is good; he notes the smell of Pond's Vanishing Cream from the girls in the choir as they form a line at the rear of the queue to communion, and the whiff of camphor balls lodged in clothes come from America and he has a great eye, and ear. In the school yard cold tea came from a Chef sauce bottle corked with a newspaper.

At school it is *A haon is a haon is a do, a do is a do is a ceathar*.

This is a rare collection of the authentic voice, both oral and literal. In 1958 in the Primary Cert one of the subjects was: You fought with Brian Boru at Clontarf, describe your adventures and feelings. Years later Joe Prior has set himself another series of questions, not about a battle but growing up in Swad as a bus driver's son. The heroic in this book is the everyday. Memory has been doing the laps with determination, and the author's research hits the page with a great deal of joy.

The title says it all; with both a nod in the right direction and a tone of acceptance- That's the way.

Dermot Healy, September 2008

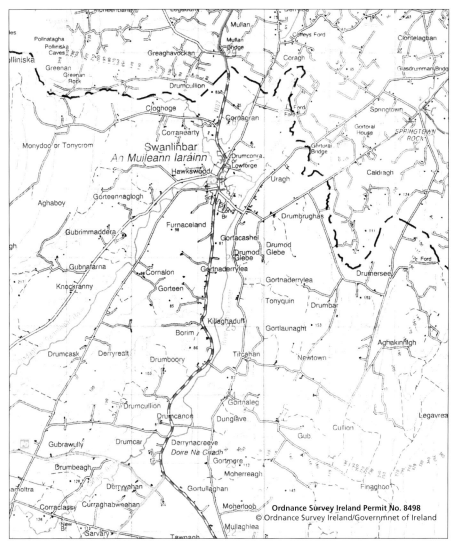

Above: Ordnance survey map of Swanlinbar and surrounding townlands

The Diamond - Swanlinbar.

BACKDROP

I grew up in the border village of Swanlinbar during the 1940's and 1950's. Since then my generation has witnessed unprecedented changes, which have completely transformed our world. I now invite you to put today's insane commercialized rush, frenetic fever and fret on hold, and join me in my time-capsule as I prepare to lever it into reverse and revisit those bygone days. But first, a few general words about the title, my privileged vantage point and the particular period.

For the uninitiated, the title, 'That's The Way', was a common greeting around my home place and surrounding areas. It was generally used when two people crossed paths for a second time in fairly quick succession and were at a loss for words. Its meaning may have been somewhat ambiguous but the speaker's intent was clear – never ever to ignore the other, whether young or old, male or female, whether he was the P.P. or a poor labourer who held up his ragged pants with binding twine, 'Hairy Ned' or with galluses (braces) connected to Bachelors' buttons (nails). For me, it encapsulates the spirit of the time and place as well as suggesting the main theme, namely the way things were back then. We took for granted this salutation and other initial ones such as 'How's she cutting?', 'How's it going?, 'That's it', 'Howaya doing ?', 'Health to yer sowl', 'A drawky day', 'A bully day', 'A soft day', 'a toppin day', 'a midlin day' 'Did you not go home yet?', 'Still here?', the more exuberant 'Ara, is it yourself that's in it?', or even that affirmative monosyllabic grunt, 'Aye'. But in to day's world with its indispensible ipods and mobile phones, where so many are absorbed with self-interest, 'hassled out of it' with the necessary busy-ness of life or as a result of the terrible culture of haste that has set in, or are naturally afraid to lift their guard in case someone would take advantage, the very quality of our lives has been diminished by their absence. In the mid 40's to early 60's, people had time for one another and would generously offer 'a day at the hay' or 'a day in the bog'. The old Irish proverb, 'Is ar scáth a chéile a mhaireann na daoine' (People live in one another's shelter) was more applicable back then when real 'characters' enjoyed a special status. Now time is in short supply and everything is for sale to the highest bidder.

Swanlinbar, situated in the old barony of Tullyhaw in North/West Cavan, nestles in a picturesque valley between the Cuilcagh (2,188 feet) and Slieve Rushen (or Russell) (1325 feet) mountains. Ben Aughlin (or Binn Aughlin), an unusual shaped mountain, formed during the last Ice Age over 12,000 years ago, maintains a discreet watch from the north-west. The village is more or less equidistant from the metropolises of Ballyconnell (10 miles), Ballinamore (11 miles) and Enniskillen (12 miles) and 7 miles from Derrylin. It is cushioned from alien influences by its satellite suburbs: Bawn, Corlough, Kinawley, Killesher and lofty Glan!

Swad, as the village is affectionately known, is beside the Ulster Walkway and built on the River Claddagh, which rises in the Cuilcagh mountains near the mystical 'Pot' of its more illustrious neighbour, the Shannon, and after an initial turbulent rush down the mountain, meanders along rather lazily through the village (except when in flood) before joining the calm and stately Blackwater near the Iron Bridge on its way to Upper Lough Erne. It is part of the parish of Kinawley, which spans two counties, Fermanagh and Cavan and two jurisdictions. Surrounding parishes in the same diocese of Kilmore include Killesher, Knockninny, Kildallon, Corlough and Templeport (1969 map).

In the 1940's and 1950's Swad's thirteen pubs, each with a six or seven day licence 'to sell Wine, Beer and Spirits for consumption on the premises' and several nearby spas ensured that the village's two hundred and fifty or so inhabitants never suffered from the throes of thirst, whatever about the pangs of hunger! Life can't have been easy in earlier times when the population tended to fluctuate. 398 dwelt there in 1831, 492 just before the Great Famine in 1841 and 402 fifty years later.

We were just a stone's throw away from the National Trust property of Florence Court House and the carboniferous limestone Marble Arch caves. Enniskillen was really our nearest large town. When growing up, we identified as much, if not more, with it as we did with any other town in our own county. It was inextricably linked to the two great northern traditions. Once the seat of the Maguires, it was captured by the English in 1607 and formally established as a town by charter of James 1 in 1612. As a garrison town, it became home to two regiments: the Inniskilling Dragoons and the Inniskilling Fusiliers. Fr. John Sullivan S.J. (1861 – 1933), 'Servant of God' and revered by many as a saint, was a student there and, like the town itself, embodied both traditions. After a brilliant academic career in the prestigious Protestant Portora Royal School (which can claim many other illustrious scholars such as Oscar Wilde, Samuel Beckett and the 'Abide with Me' hymn writer, Henry Francis Lyte), he later embraced his mother's Catholic faith and became a Jesuit priest in 1900. In more recent times, Enniskillen has come to be associated in the minds of many with the bomb explosion that killed eleven innocent people there on Remembrance Day, November, 1987.

The Swanlinbar area itself has a long and illustrious history. We know that an army from the West Oriel kingdom of Fermanagh fought here in the twelfth century. It seems there was fairly regular conflict between the Mac Uidhir and the Mac Samhradháin rulers of Teallach Eachach or Tullyhaw. They say that the ghost of Donn Carrach Mac Uidhir (who established Mac Uidhir supremacy in Fermanagh before he died early in the 14th.century) still haunts the slopes of 'Binn'.

We have authentic evidence that St. Naile, a 6th.century saint and friend of Colmcille, founded a church in Kinawley- an area previously associated with Saint Rabharnog- and that St. Tigernach established a Christian foundation one mile south of the village of Swanlinbar in 806A.D. The latter site is marked by the East wall of a 15thcentury church in the local cemetery of Killaghaduff (Cill Acaidh Dubh).

The baronial map of 1609 shows a round tower close by and it's likely that there was a monastery here as well. During Penal times people worshipped in a Mass garden in this area and at Mass Rocks dotted around the parish at Drumbennis, Teesnaughton, Drumersee and Doon. Towards the end of the eighteenth century, when penal legislation relaxed somewhat, a thatched church was built in the Mass Garden at Killaghaduff and this served until a new church opened in the village itself in 1828.

A well preserved window in the East Wall of the 15th century church at Killaghaduff

This was built on a site leased from the local landlord, Major Burrowes of Stradone. The rent became the subject of much controversy over the years until the matter was finally settled in 1940. After Fr. Whelan P.P. refused to pay up in 1868, the Sheriff arrived to seize the property in 1869 only to be met by more than 1,000 men armed with pitchforks and such weapons! The church was renovated in 1927 and again in 1959 but was destroyed by a bomb during 'The Troubles' on December 8, 1974. Its replacement, a beautiful modern structure with floor sloping towards the altar, designed by Hubert Duffy, was rededicated on August 15, 1978.

The festival of Lugnasa was celebrated on Ben Aughlin (or Binn Eachlainn). Every year on the last Sunday in July (called 'Binn', Bilberry, Donagh Deireannach or Garland Sunday) people gathered here, picked bilberries and enjoyed themselves with dancing, wrestling, music and song. These annual gatherings filtered out completely in the 1930's. From early Christian times a somewhat similar ritual, without the bilberries but interspersed with Christian prayers, was repeated at Cloch na dTuras, a huge stone overlooking Kinawley and at Tobar Naile nearby.

Swanlinbar was a centre of iron manufacture for several centuries until the supply of local timber for the initial smelting in Furnaceland and subsequent refining process near Lunney's Ford in Drumconra (renamed Lowforge) ran out around 1760. Dean Swift (1667 – 1745) in his 'On Barbarous Denominations in Ireland' paid his own 'tribute' to the place when he noted,

'There is a famous town, where the worst iron in the kingdom is made, and it is called Swandlingbar: the original of which name I shall explain, lest the antiquaries of future ages might be at a loss to derive it. It was a most witty conceit of four gentlemen, who ruined themselves with the iron project. Sw stands for Swift, And for Sanders, Ling for Darling and Bar for Barry.'

The 'Swift' referred to in the quote was Goodwin, uncle of the famous Dean, who wrote much of his celebrated classic, 'Gulliver's Travels' in Virginia. Goodwin and his three business colleagues, Robert Sanders, Richard Barry and Richard Darling, managed the iron project from 1682 until it collapsed in 1728. By the middle of the nineteenth century the place was generally listed as 'Swanlinbar' but villagers and frequent visitors continued to use the abbreviated version of the old name (Swadlingbar), referring to it as 'Swad'. Not surprisingly, its Irish name is Muileann Iarainn (The Iron Mill).

The village also had its own tannery. 'Tannery House' was situated in what came to be known as the 'Tanyard Lane' and holes where the leather was steeped were only filled in during the early days of the twentieth century.

Tradition has it that Lord Cole from Florencecourt and his Glenawley Yeomanry, who fought on the 15,000 strong British side under Lord Cornwallis at the Battle of Ballinamuck in Co. Longford on September 8, 1798, celebrated their victory over the 1,500 Irish and French soldiers by stealing cattle on the way home and rounded up their considerable herd in Swanlinbar. Whatever about the authenticity of this story, we do know from the 'Postchaise Companion' of 1786 that Swad was famous for its iron, sulphur and magnesium mineral waters. These minerals come from the rock of the Cuilcagh mountains. Carried along by the water, they percolate through the porous rocks and shale to surface at the various springs. These, located at Mullan, Uragh/Gortoral and Dromod Glebe/Drumbrughas, were said to be 'alterative and diaphoretic and highly efficacious as a restorative from debility'!

By 1775, Swanlinbar, which was situated on the old Dublin to Enniskillen coach road, had become a fashionable resort, rivalling places like Bath and Harrogate in England, Spa in Belgium (the place that gave its name to thermal resorts worldwide) and a whole host of others in Ireland - Lucan in West Dublin, Castleconnell in Co. Limerick, Kilmeadon in Co. Waterford, Leixlip in Co. Kildare, Mallow in Co. Cork, Ballyspellin and Spa in Kerry and Lisdoonvarna (the only spa town left in Ireland) in county Clare, and was frequented by visitors from Dublin and large concourses of neighbouring gentry. Henry Grattan, First Minister of the old Irish Parliament (Grattan's Parliament 1775 – 1800), Sir Walter Scott (1771-1832), the great poet and historical novelist and Dean Swift were just three of its many distinguished visitor.

The holiday season lasted from April to September. Dr. Peter Livingstone in his classic, 'The Fermanagh Story', tells us that lodgings here cost well-off adults 8s. a day. Their servants were charged a half-crown (2/6). Mr. Castle's Spa Hotel in Uragh was the most prestigious. It could boast of a coach house close by at Gortoral, ornamental gardens, walks through the woods and entertainment such as horse racing, which could be viewed from its balconies during the height of the season. There were lesser hotels in the village itself but many visitors opted to remain in their coaches. The tourist guide for Dublin visitors to Mr. Castle's gave a rough outline of a day's programme:

PROGRAMME

6a.m - 9a.m - Visit to well for regular drinks and intermittent exercise

10a.m - Breakfast in pump-house

1p.m - A few more libations at well

3p.m - Return to hotel to dress for dinner

4p.m - Dinner

10p.m - Retire for the night without supper

The last of the Spring wine!
Above left: Mullan Spa with Ben Aughlin in the background. Above right: Dromod (Terry Maguire's) Sulphur Spa,

You were advised to 'be temperate in wine and to drink as little Chinese tea as possible'! Can you imagine any of Sean Quinn's present-day guests in nearby 'Slieve Russell' settling for such a package! However, I would recommend a visit to the Dromod spa (known locally as 'Terry Maguire's Spa') which is situated south east of the village. It is still accessible and its sulphur-rich water is supposed to be good for rheumatism. Just don't bank on a miracle. Like good whiskey, the potion could possibly make you well, if sick, but could well make you sick, if well! The spring at Uragh is rich in magnesium. People reckon it is good for stomach pains but these may have subsided before you find the well!

A fire burned twenty two houses on the west side of Swad in 1786, killing 20 people and injuring many more. While this did irreparable damage to the resort and was a terrible body-blow to the 398 inhabitants, its fate had already been sealed. Nine years earlier Viscount Enniskillen built Bundoran Lodge (now known as Homefield House) as his summer residence and set the fashion trend among the leisured classes of going on holidays to the Donegal resort instead. Here they could enjoy 'the splendid sea-bathing and intensely bracing and invigorating health-giving air'. By the time the G.N.R. linked Bundoran to all the major population centres in 1866, it was certainly well and truly established as one of the premier resorts in the country. In fact, it was hailed as the 'Brighton of Ireland'. The railway adverts encouraged people to 'Bathe, Bask and Bronze at Bundoran' with its golden strand, where 'sunlight danced on its rippling waves'. What chance had poor old Swad with its humble spas? Some did continue to visit until around 1850 and the village could still boast of having its own constabulary police station, Penny post and petty sessions on alternative Wednesdays and a weekly market on Saturday for the sale of oates, potatoes, butter, eggs, fowl etc. However, it suffered a further blow when its tannery in the Tanyard Lane, famous around the early 1800's, also went out of business.

To make matters worse, it was 'passed over' when railway stations were being allocated and so it gradually became something of a backwater. In fact, as far as non-natives were concerned, the place, like Rip Van Winkle, went into a deep sleep after the tourists left and didn't waken from its slumber until border smuggling 'took off' during the war years, or at least until the I.R.A. put it back on the map during their short lived campaign in the late 50's. Radio listeners at that time heard newsreaders repeatedly announce that 'in Swanlinbar, the Gardai were very active but no arrests were made'! The West Cavan region suffered badly during the terrible mid 19th century famine and lost at least 18% of its population to emigration between 1936 and 1951. Swanlinbar, in particular, missed out on any worthwhile government support over the years and most of its young inhabitants were forced to seek a living elsewhere.

Swanlinbar didn't rank highly in terms of commerce or industry. The border, which separated it from its northern hinterland, inhibited economic growth and the place suffered both physically and psychologically from the northern conflicts. Viewed by some as a kind of 'no man's land', it was seldom or never listed in the tourist brochures with the likes of Sheelin, Shannon or Shantemon. Robert Praeger in his book, 'The Way that I Went', referred to 'the long north-west arm of Cavan from the Erne to Belcoo' as 'a remote region, little known to visitors whether scientific or otherwise, full of lakes in the Erne watershed, rather grim and lonely towards the north west'! We were even omitted from most booklets on place-names.

Cutting 'the long acre' 'neath Ben Aughlin's brow. Photo Louis Morrison

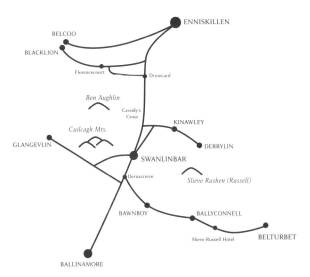

Swanlinbar and environs

The great Ballymena travel writer, Richard Hayworth, writing about the Slieve Rushen region of Swad, was a little more magnanimous. He noted in his 'Border Foray' that 'it was a countryside rich in folklore and legend and one inhabited by a kindly people who are always ready to lend a helping hand to a stranger or welcome him to the family hearth for 'a bit of crack'. Christopher Winn in his book, 'I Never Knew That about Ireland' referred to the fact that 'in the eighteenth century, Swanlinbar was one of Ireland's most popular spa towns, noted for the sulphur and magnesium in its waters'.

However, when I went to St. Patrick's College, Cavan, a professor there nicknamed 'Smigs', on eliciting my place of origin, announced in front of the whole class that it was a place inhabited by 'mountainy men with boughalauns growing out of their ears!' Was I embarrassed? I should mention in passing that the good professor was later sent by his bishop to shepherd the same 'mountainy' flock! He proved to be a good and very popular pastor before being laid to rest alongside the church.

When fellow students in that hallowed institution, who hailed from the more yuppy and wealthier eastern part of the county, really wanted to 'wind us up' or 'turn the screw', they would poke fun at the entrance signs to our village which read 'SLOW THROUGH SWANLINBAR', insinuating that these had been erected to ensure that no 'passer by' missed the place through the blink of an eye! They referred to our beloved part as an 'oul bog at the back of beyond', 'the last place God created' or worse still 'the arse-hole of Cavan'! They claimed that our main street got mainer the further up you went! Then, like Kavanagh, on hearing others belittle his beloved 'Shancoduff', 'my heart was sore'.

Later on, they too would have to share our suffering when people like Mr. Toibin and Co., would tell the world how 'odious good' we were 'at turning a buck', that we were a shower of 'cute hoors', all with our First Holy money stashed away and fully intact, that those working in the mint had to put several sides on the old 50p coin so that it could be wrenched from a Cavan man's grasp, that a certain town square in the county is now a triangle because its inhabitants refused to pay rates on the fourth side!

While I haven't resided permanently in my home village of Swanlinbar for over thirty six years, it still has a very special place in my heart. I have some wonderful memories of my growing up there and know how my sense of belonging to that neck of the woods and the love and support I received there have sustained me through the years. Even to day when asked where I am from, I automatically refer to it and whenever the Breffni Blues take the field, I never have any problem knowing where my allegiance lies.

Many people didn't find life easy during the 40's and 50's. Apart from the negative effects of what was proceeding on the international stage, we had lots of problems on the home front. In 1946, 61.3% of households did not have piped water. During the early 40's and even later, there were severe housing shortages and poor infrastructure, scarcity of basic items such as butter, bread, tea, flour, clothes, coal, gas and matches and the consequent need for rationing.

'Bless de Valera and Sean Mac Entee
Bless their brown bread and their half ounce of tea'!

Things did not return to anything approaching normal after the war until around 1949. Even then there was 'a palpable mood of despondency' (Ken Whittaker). No wonder. Ireland had unstable government, a T.B.epidemic, mass unemployment and what impinged most of all on places like Swad, mass emigration, which sapped the general dynamism and spirit of the community. The population of County Cavan fell from 70,355 to 59,954 between 1946 and 1961 and didn't begin to stabilise until the Lemass Era. The 1955 census showed the population of the Republic as a whole at its lowest level. Swanlinbar, that could boast of having 402 inhabitants in 1891 (according to Slater's Directory), now had less than 300.

Mechanisation was beginning to reduce the need for farm labourers and small West Cavan farms could only support a single son. Young girls, who worked as shop assistants or as 'home helps', were paid a mere pittance. Labouring men employed on local projects didn't fare all that much better. What could a family of ten to twelve children do, especially if they depended on a 'mixed' farm with its three or four cows, a sow, a donkey (the 'poor man's horse'), some sheep and a few hens? With no industries nearby, no 'call from Dev' in the post, and a huge demand for labourers, trainee nurses etc. in the major British cities, it was inevitable that many would opt to leave the 'nest' and pay the £3.50s.one-way fare for the mail boat to Holyhead or 'cattle boat' to Liverpool as soon as they reached working age.

It was a traumatic time for parents and children. Emigration heralded the disintegration of a family and drained the very life blood of a community. Apart from this, can you imagine the anguish and the trauma some of these young people from places such as Aughandiagh (the field of the two ravens), Althacullion (the cliff of the holly), Gortnaleg (the field of the legs or hollows) or Aughnakelly (the hag's field) must have experienced when they disembarked at London's Euston station or tried to pass a lonely Sunday afternoon in some park in London, Birmingham, Manchester, Liverpool or Glasgow, not to speak of more distant climes. Still, they settled in as best they could. Many of the girls trained as nurses or worked as 'domestics' while the boys toiled away in factories or laboured with Wimpey, Mc Alpine or Green Murphy.

Some spent their free time in pubs such as 'The Crown' in Crickelwood, danced their Saturday nights away in 'The Blarney Club', 'The Hammersmith Palais', 'The Garryowen' or ' The Galtymore' and dreamt of eventually 'going back yonder'. They never forgot those at home. Their regular registered letters and ten shilling postal orders ensured that those left behind didn't want for the basic necessities of life and that a new television, fridge or extra bed made life that little bit more comfortable. For a few years, some did return for a week or two during the summer – often to help out with the hay – but after their parents passed away, they came to realise that there was nothing to return to. Their dreams died and many married and settled down in the Camden Towns and Kilburns of the '50's.

There were of course other unpalatable aspects. While we may not like to admit it, we Irish were quite inward looking and puritanical with a rather Jansenistic attitude to sexuality. Any deviation from the social norms was frowned upon and Swad, like every other rural village, had its own quota of 'squinting windows'.

'Unfortunate girls', whose children were born out of wedlock, were viewed as shameful and often treated as 'outcasts' while the children themselves were more or less banished, lost all contact with their parents and were penalised under the law with regard to succession rights.

There were 6,000 poor and vulnerable urchins in the industrial schools and institutions, thanks to the fact that society and the State failed to live up to their obligations. As a result, the religious, often without the benefit of adequate training and resources, not to speak of their own personal inadequacies, were left to 'carry the can' and take the 'flak'.

Some wives had to stay behind and fend for large families while their husbands sought work and sustenance abroad. Their heroism prompted popular poet, Brendan Kennelly, to call them 'The Trojan Women'.

Nor can we forget the many incidents of clerical and lay sexual abuse, including some horrific paedophile activities, most of which went undetected until relatively recently.

The Catholic Church (together with Fianna Fail and the G.A.A) had things pretty well 'sewn up' in the '50's. While it showed great concern for the spiritual welfare of its people and made a notable contribution to the health and educational services and indeed to the social and cultural life of the nation, as well as serving the needs of those in underdeveloped countries, you could hardly say it was particularly intent on lifting the weary spirits of its flock. In stark contrast to ancient Irish traditional practice and the mix of piety and fun that was such a feature of the 'pattern days', nothing in the 'here and now' seemed worthy of celebration. Its chapel-centred rituals tended to focus almost exclusively on the next life. They were there to facilitate redemption and ensure that you escaped the clutches of the quare fellow with the hoofs, ever anxious to capture you for his bonfire below! Emphasis on sin, especially on sins of the flesh, led to sexual repression and induced guilt, fear and personal scrupulosity. In fact, apart from highlighting the dangers associated with it, sex was a taboo subject and there was never even a hint that if God created anything more pleasurable, He kept it to Himself!

With the great mass of Irish people crowding into Catholic churches, no shortage of priests to serve them and the Church's 'special position' enshrined in the Constitution of our relatively new State, a rather triumphant stance was discernible. Attitudes towards other religions and the perceived position regarding salvation for those outside the Catholic fold were less than enlightened. The ban on Catholics entering Trinity College, introduced by Archbishop McQuaide in 1944, was symbolic of the excessive fear of contamination that existed at the time.

While the majority of the clergy were holy, exemplary and selfless 'men of God' and the local newspapers' somewhat hackneyed description of a P.P. as 'a pious, humble man, universally loved' was generally apt, some encouraged a rather haughty 'cap in hand' approach, kept ordinary punters 'in tow' with the power of 'the cloth' and on occasions, humiliated them from the pulpit. As far as they were concerned, there were three commandments, 'Pray, Pay and Obey! While the Church wasn't solely responsible for the demise of Dr. Noel Browne's visionary, free, non-means tested 'Mother and Child' welfare scheme, its somewhat blinkered view didn't help.

All in all, it is no wonder then that so many were glad to leave the austerity of the 1940's and 1950's behind and welcome the new idealistic Irish American President, John F. Kennedy (1917 – 1963), with his youthful vigour, his charm and contagious optimism, our own new Taoiseach, Sean Lemass (1899 – 1971), with his programme for Economic Expansion, his 'emphasis on efficiency, international competitiveness, experimentation and commitment to the mixed economy' (Brian Farrell), his promise of 100,000 new jobs within five years and belief that 'the rising tide would lift all boats'. There was the lovable new Pope, John XXIII (Angelo Giuseppe Roncalli 1881 – 1963), who would call a second Vatican Council (1962 – 1965) in order to pull back the curtains and let in the light.

> *Letting in light was the good Pope's intent,*
> *But he hadn't in mind Gaybo's extent.*
> *De Valera retired to his Arus mansion,*
> *And Lemass was on fire with 'Economic Expansion'.*
> *'Twas the time to stick on your Hucklebuck shoes,*
> *And line up with the hopefuls in the ballroom queues.*

Right across the board there were indeed discernible signs of transition. At home, the Reynolds brothers were beginning to open up ballrooms such as the Cloudland in Rooskey, Co. Roscommon (September 1957) and the Roseland in Moate, Co, Westmeath (in '59). 'The Wonderland' in Bawnboy, 'Fenaghville' (later christened 'The Ivy Leaf'), 'The Silver Slipper' in Enniskillen and 'The Merryland' in Clones and other 'breeze block basilicas' would all follow suit. The 'Clipper Carlton' with their 'Juke Box Saturday night', Brendan Boyer's 'Royal Showband', the 'Drifters', 'Miami', 'Cadets', 'Dixies' and our own Sean Gilheaney's 'Red Sunbeam' and 'Carnegie' with James 'Jazzy' Mc Govern on drums would start 'packing them in' and with their 'Good night, God bless and safe home' dismissal 'send the crowds away sweatin'.

In the world at large, modern inventions, new techniques and previously unknown materials were being introduced. Other ideals and new values were taking shape. The gloomy war years eventually gave way to a climate of optimism. Life became more colourful, fashion more cheerful. In fact, colour was the principal characteristic of the new lifestyle. Initially, innovation and luxury goods may have been treated with some suspicion but this soon changed. Radio and television introduced the outside world into our living rooms and increasing mobility broadened horizons. Things would never be quite the same again!

Despite the austerity, the doom and the gloom associated with the 40's and 50's, for many of us growing up in the border village, surprising though it may seem, it was a time of innocence and wonder, a time of contentment, laughter and fun, a kind of "Christmas Childhood". I will now try to re-capture some of that magic before 'CRAFT' (Can't Remember A Flipping Thing!) sets in!

I know that the late Spike Milligan didn't like looking back. He said that it hurt his neck! I just hope my reminiscing will conjure up many more good memories for you and will not have any such adverse effect! We can't turn back the clock so why not wind it up again.

Above: CAVAN ALL IRELAND FOOTBALL CHAMPIONS 1947. Photo taken at the All Ireland semi-final against Roscommon.
Back Row: John Wilson, Colm McDyer, Edwin Carolan, Tony Tighe, Peter Donohoe, Terry Sheridan, Eunan Tiernan,
Jim Deignan, Phil Brady, Hughie Smith (Secretary), Brian O'Reilly, Paddy Smith.
Front Row: Joe Stafford, Bill Doonan, Simon Deignan, John Joe O'Reilly (Captain), T. P. O'Reilly, Mick Higgins, Val Gannon,
Owen Roe McGovern, Dan Denneher, (Missing P. J. Duke injured). Photo coutesy of Frank Burke

Cavan's Golden Era
1947 and all that

I think it appropriate to begin my reminiscing by referring to that legendary broadcaster, Micheál O'Hehir, since it was his commentary on the famous Cavan/Kerry All-Ireland final in the Polo Grounds in New York on Sunday 14th.of September 1947 that formed my very earliest recollection and he himself was synonymous with Sunday afternoon in our house during all my childhood years.

I can recall my parents and aunt huddled around the crackling wireless in the sitting-room that night in '47 as the sound came and went just like the Kerry lead. I didn't know then all that I know now, as the story of that game was repeated over and over again for years afterwards and I dare say 'twas embellished in the telling. Several ingredients added spice to the occasion. Kerry, chief curators of Sam, were our opponents, the location was New York, the greatest city in the world, and Owen Roe Mc Govern, one of our own, was included in the Cavan panel. Locals were particularly enamoured at his inclusion because of a widely held belief that West Cavan footballers did not always get 'cothrom na féinne' when it came to selecting the county team.

The idea of playing the game in America was proposed by Canon Hamilton from Clare who, like another strong advocate, John Kerry O' Donnell of the New York Gaelic board, felt 'the thrill and joy and exaltation of an All-Ireland final' would help to promote the game there. It was the centenary year of the Great Famine and Irish teams hadn't been to the States for some time on account of the war. Many of our exiles too had been cut off from home during those years. Despite strong opposition from many quarters – ironically, some of the most vehement from Cavan – his motion got the approval of Congress.

Cavan, in actual fact, were lucky to make it to the final that year as they had great trouble beating neighbours, Monaghan, in the first round of the Ulster championship. The Farney men, with great players such as Eugene Mc Donald, Paddy and Ollie O' Rourke and class forward, Hughie Mc Kearney, were level on six occasions before Cavan scraped through in the replay by a mere two points. They went on to defeat Armagh by fifteen points and then got revenge on the reigning Ulster champions, Antrim, the team that foiled their bid for eight successive Ulster titles when they defeated them by 2-8 to 1-7 in the 1946 final. In the All-Ireland semi-final they had four points to spare over the red hot favourites, Roscommon (2 – 4 to 0 – 6), thanks to a fine scoring spree by Peter Donohoe who chalked up 1-4. Tony Tighe got the other goal. The 'Indo' referred to 'the courage with which players sailed into each other to take the hard knocks that awaited them, and to the miraculous save by Dolan from Stafford when the latter seemed certain to score and the enthusiasm which followed the close.' The 'Irish Times' noted that 'Cavan's thrust and speed merited victory. They were a dashing side, splendidly fit and they finished a grueling hour just as they began.' The Connaught champions were told by their mentors before the game to have their passports ready! In fairness, they were unlucky to have a Jack Mc Quillan goal disallowed and this didn't help their cause.

The broadcast of the New York final, due to take place in the Polo Grounds, home of the New York Giants baseball team, was in some doubt until the last minute but fortunately it got the 'go-ahead'. My father and many others throughout the land had their wet batteries on the ready as news filtered through that the teams had arrived safely in America. Some, including Cavan's Bill Doonan had sailed from Cobh on the Cunard's 'Mauritania' on Tuesday 2 September. Bill, who had served in the R.A.F. during World War 2 and lost two of his toes in the process, reckoned he had enough of flying! Other players and officials as well as Mitchel Cogley of the 'Independent', Anna Kelly of the 'Irish Press' and 27-year-old commentator, Micheál O' Hehir, travelled from Shannon on a TWA Skymaster.

There was a wonderful build-up to the game itself – a ticker-tape parade down Broadway, a reception by the Mayor, Bill O'Dwyer of Mayo, a stadium inspection on the Friday and finally, a special Mass celebrated by Cardinal Francis Spellman in St. Patrick's Cathedral on the morning of the big day.

Kerry were firm favourites. They had appeared in seven of the previous ten All Irelands, winning five of them. Cavan, during the same period, reached only three and lost those three in 1937,'43 and '45. The predictions seemed to be accurate as Kerry's Gega O'Connor scored a point and Batt Garvey a goal before Peter Donohoe opened Cavan's account with a point from a free after six minutes. Kerry were soon back on fire! Eddie Dowling soloed from centrefield, sidestepped five opponents and gave Gannon no chance as he sent the ball to the corner of the Cavan net for what was probably the best goal of the game. It was also to be his last kick. Gega O'Connor and Garvey rifled the same net on two other occasions but not before Wexford referee, Martin O'Neill, had sounded his whistle. Some biased Kerrymen to this day maintain that O'Neill blew because he was afraid there would be a Kerry rout and that the spectators wouldn't get value for their money! Of course, some also insist that the final result would have been different if more of their players had travelled across by plane to this game that should never have been played in New York in the first instance! You just can't win! Whatever the story, Kerry were eight points in front after fifteen minutes and Cavan heads among the 34,941 attendance (considerably less than the 50,000 expected) were beginning to sag.

A few positional changes, however, caused the tide to turn. P.J.Duke began to mark the Kerry ace, Batt Garvey, and Tony Tighe and Mick Higgins were moved to midfield. Kerry suffered a serious set back when Eddie Dowling had to go off with an injury after falling heavily on the rock hard ground. This was the real turning point in the game. Peter Donohoe (who scored eight points on the day and was afterwards titled the 'Babe Ruth of Gaelic football' by the American press) chipped over a few points from frees and Joe Stafford and Mick Higgins shook the Kerry net to put their team one point ahead in the twenty eighth minute. At half-time the score stood: Cavan 2-5 Kerry 2-4. It was still anyone's game.

After the resumption, Kerry 'left no stone unturned' but to a man, Cavan played superbly, especially half backs Simon Deignan (who, incidentally, refereed the Munster final that year), John Joe O'Reilly, their captain, and P.J.Duke. The terrible heat (98 F) affected the older Kerry team more than their younger challengers but still Cavan only held a one-point lead with five minutes remaining. After that, Donohoe (a free), Phil Brady and New York-born Mick Higgins

A youthful looking Micheal O' Hehir (27) with John Joe, Bill O' Brien (aide to Bill O' Dwyer, Mayor of New York) and Mitchel Cogley in New York in '47. (Photo-Cavan County Museum, Ballyjamesduff)

Cardinal Francis Spellman greeting captains, J.J. O' Reilly, D.Lyne, other players and officials outside St. Patrick's Cathedral, New York on the morning of the big game. (Photo – Sr. Elizabeth O' Rourke, Sligo)

went on to give them a four point advantage. The final score was Cavan 2-11 Kerry 2-7. Tim Brosnan almost saved Kerry's bacon near the end but fortunately for the Breffni men, his rasper hit the cross-bar.

The teams on that famous day were as follows:

Cavan – *Vincent Gannon, Bill Doonan, Brian O'Reilly, Paddy Smith, John Wilson, John Joe O'Reilly (Capt.), Simon Deignan, P.J. Duke, Phil Brady, Tony Tighe, Mick Higgins, Columba Mc Dwyer, Joe Stafford, Peter Donohoe and T.P.O' Reilly.*

Kerry – *D. O'Keeffe, D.Lyne (Capt.), J. Keohane, P. Brosnan, J.Lyne, W. Casey, E. Walsh, E. Dowling, E. O'Connor, E. O' Sullivan, D. Kavanagh, B. Garvey, F. O' Keefe, T. O'Connor and P. Kennedy. Subs. – W. O'Donnell for E. Dowling, M. Finucane for E. Walsh, T. Brosnan for W. O'Donnell and G. Teehan for P. Kennedy.*

The game was supposed to start at 3.30p.m. (8.30p.m. Irish time) but it didn't get going until 3.38p.m. owing to a host of pre-match introductions. Greetings home to Ireland by Mayor O'Dwyer and the affable G.A.A. President, Dan o'Rourke (one of the main architects of Roscommon's rise in the early '40's) and prolonged discussion on possible tactics in the Kerry dressing room at half-time meant it couldn't end as scheduled. Poor Micheál O'Hehir, conscious of the fact that he was the link between this historic match and the thousands of football followers at home, became frantic as he feared his broadcast would be cut off at a vital moment when Cavan were leading by a single point. He begged whoever was in charge of the wireless lines to give him the extra few minutes. Fortunately his request was granted.

The American press gave the whole thing great coverage. Louis Effrat of the New York Times wrote as follows: 'It was a heart-warming finish. The teams, after knocking the stuffing out of each other, rushed over, not to throw a final punch but to shake hands and congratulate each other – a magnificent gesture.' The only real criticism came from Harold Rosenthal of the Herald Tribune. There's always one! He noted that seats costing 2 dollars and 40 cents would have been available at a similar event in Dublin for a mere 50 cents! Since then the G.A.A. in its wisdom has taken steps to rectify that situation!

The September 20th edition of the 'Anglo Celt' devoted four large headings to its match report

> CAVAN'S GLORIOUS VICTORY
> KERRY MASTERED IN MEMORABLE GAME
> WONDER FOOTBALL WINS AMERICAN ACCLAIM
> ENTHUSIASTIC SCENES AT POLO GROUNDS NEW YORK

Elsewhere the same paper reported that 'in Cavan town, fires were lit at several points and cheering crowds marched through the streets until long after midnight.' The Swad news noted that 'Swanlinbar's reaction to Cavan's football victory was to rush into the streets when the result was announced and people cheered as never before. Men who had hitherto been silent became loquacious, whilst others, normally regarded as sensible, displayed symptoms of light-headedness!' A large crowd had gathered to listen to the match over a loudspeaker in Wood's Hall. These were mainly the people Cissie was referring to in her bulletin. Naturally, the dance, scheduled to take place at the same venue, had to be postponed for some time until the excitement died down.

Dan O' Rourke (Roscommon), President of the G.A.A., Comdt. John Joe O' Reilly (Cavan captain), Sean T. O' Ceallaigh, President of Ireland, Dinny Lyne (Kerry captain), Bean Ui Ceallaigh and Eamon de Valera, Taoiseach, at the Presidential reception for the Cavan and Kerry teams in Aras an Uachtarain. (Photo- Sr. Elizabeth O' Rourke, Sligo)

The teams enjoyed a meal after the game in the Commodore Hotel and continued to get deferential treatment until they set sail from New York on the 'Queen Mary' on the following Wednesday 24, September. Eight days later, they arrived in Southampton. There were further receptions there and later in Dún Laoghaire, in the Mansion House, in Áras an Uachtaráin and in the Gresham Hotel where John Joe was presented with the Sam Maguire cup. They were also paraded through O' Connell Street by the Artane Boys' Band. Still, the best had yet to come. Well over 15,000 delirious Cavan men and women greeted the players with tumultuous applause as they drove behind fifteen bands through the streets of the county town. Nothing quite like it had ever been seen here before. Swanlinbar G.F.C. was represented at the team reception by S. Young (Chairman), J. Mc Govern (V.C.), S. Mc Hugh (Sec.), H. Cullen (Treas.), J. Young (Captain) and W. Lynch.

Swanlinbar marked the occasion in its own special way. West Cavan men, T.P.O'Reilly and Owen Roe Mc Govern got a hero's welcome as the Templeport band led the parade through the village on the following Wednesday night. Torchlights, prepared earlier that evening in Woods's yard, helped to create a real carnival atmosphere, and the whole spectacle must have given great satisfaction to the organizers: Seamus and Paddy Mc Hugh, Hubie Dolan, James and Hugh Owney and Andy Kelly. T.P. and Owen Roe were guests of honour at a celebratory meal, hosted by Swad G.A.A. in the Spa Hotel that night. Here, Very Rev. Canon Kelly P.P. read the address of welcome The whole occasion went into the annals as 'A Night to Remember'.

Some may recall 1947 as the year England beat Portugal 10-0 (with Tommy Layton and Stan Mortens each scoring 4 goals), the year Sugar Ray Robinson retained his World Welterweight title by knocking out Jimmy Doyle, the year that Fred Daly from Northern Ireland won the British Open or as 'The Year of The Big Snow', but in Cavan Sam anaesthetized most, if not all, of those events. It was and still is fondly remembered as 'The Year of The Polo Grounds'.

Cavan were involved in many other classics during those halcyon years. In 1943, they defeated Cork in the semi-final by a single point (1-8 to 1-7) and went on to draw with Roscommon (1-6 apiece) before losing out (2-7 to 2-2) in the re-played final. They lost to Roscommon again in '44, their cause hampered by the absence of three players due to suspensions. They qualified for the final yet again in 1945 by defeating Wexford (1-4 to 0-5) but this time had to succumb (2-5 to 0-7) to Cork. They drew with the Rebels in the 1948 National League final (2-11 to 3-8) and got sweet revenge for '45 when they came out on top (5-9 to 2-8) in the re-play to win the county's only League title. Later that same year they accounted for Down, Monaghan and finally Antrim in the Ulster final before going on to challenge Louth in the All-Ireland semi-final. Favoured by a particularly strong wind in the first half, they went in at the interval leading by 1-10 to 0-1. However, two goals by Mick Hardy of Louth and one each from his team-mates, Fagan and Mooney, put them back in contention leaving just a single point deficit. Just then 'Babe Ruth' himself added two more to settle the issue.

Cavan had a somewhat similar experience against Mayo in the final. 74, 000 watched this game and it is estimated that 20,000 others had to be turned away. Mayo were quite confident going into this game, having beaten Kerry by 13 points to 3 in the semi-final but Cavan, favoured by a strong breeze in the first half, led 3-2 to 0-0 at the interval. Tony Tighe had an

John Joe with first year student, Peter Shaffrey, from Baileborough, in the Sam Maguire
cup, when he visited his old Alma Mater, St. Patrick's College, Cavan.
Photo Cavan County Museum, Ballyjamesduff

outstanding game. His fielding was superb, he scored a goal with each foot and his pass to Victor Sherlock led to Cavan's third goal. A Mick Higgins goal early in the second half put Cavan further ahead but Mayo clawed their way back into the game. John Joe O' Reilly had to go off injured and Mongey and Carney began to take over at centre field. A Padraig Carney goal from the penalty spot left it 4-4 to 4-1 and later Carney, Mongey and Mulderrig points evened things up at 4-4 apiece. Just when a replay seemed inevitable, Peter Donohoe once more came to the rescue with his fine match- winning point. There was some dispute with regard to Mick Higgins standing too close when Padraig Carney was taking a late fourteen yards free but the referee deemed everything in order and Michael O' Hehir, never stuck for an apt comment, reminded his listeners that captain John Joe would be taking Sam, like Paddy Reilly, back to Ballyjamesduff!

The '48 team was as follows: *J.D. Benson, W. Doonan, B.O' Reilly, P.Smith, P.J. Duke, J.J. O' Reilly, S. Duignan, P. Brady, V. Sherlock (1-1), T. Tighe (2 goals), M. Higgins (1 goal), J.J. Cassidy, J. Stafford, P.Donohoe (0-4), E. Carolan. Sub. O.R.Mc Govern for the injured J.J. O' Reilly.*

1948 was probably the most successful year for Cavan football. Not only did the county team win the National League and All-Ireland titles but St. Patrick's College captured the Mc Rory Cup and went on to qualify for the All-Ireland where sadly, they were beaten in the end by St. Mel's College, Longford (4-7 to 3-3)

In 1949 there was a special commemoration in Cavan to mark the 300th.anniversary of the death of Eoghan Roe O'Neill (1590 – 1649). It was hoped that this would coincide with a three-in-a-row for the county but it was not to be. Cavan had a comfortable win over Tyrone, beat Antrim by four points and just scraped past Armagh on a score line of 1-7 to 1-6. They were also lucky to pip Cork in the All-Ireland semi-final (0-10 to 2-3) but eventually lost to first-time winners, Meath, by 1-10 to 1-6.

However, they got their own back to some extent when they defeated the Royal county in the National League Home final in 1950. Unfortunately, they had two goals disallowed in the first half of the final 'proper' against a particularly robust New York team, who ran out winners by 2-8 to 0-12. Both sides finished the game with fourteen men. It was a devastating blow to a team that had lost the Ulster final to Armagh just one week earlier.

Antrim got the upper hand in 1951, but Cavan were back on the winning trail again in '52. Still they were very lucky to come out on top in a thrilling Ulster semi-final against the champions, Antrim, who had such polished performers as Kevin Armstrong, Harry O'Neill and Sean Gallagher. A controversial penalty, converted by Cavan's John Joe Cassidy was probably the decisive score in this match. Monaghan with Percy Mc Cooey, Ollie O' Rourke, John Rice and Hughie Mc Kearney in great form, also gave them 'a run for their money' in the Ulster final. In the All-Ireland semi-final that year, Cavan scored five points in the last six minutes to pip Cork by a single point – a truly remarkable achievement. The final score was 0-10 to 2-3. Mick Higgins had one of his best hours while J.J. Cassidy got the vital late points. Fortunately for the Breffni men, the Munster champions were short two of their best players that day, Eamon Young and Con Mc Grath. Then in the final, they scored 2-4 to Meath's 1-7. Paddy Meegan put the Royals ahead 1-7 to 2-3 late in the second half. Meath were still in front one minute into extra time but Edwin Carolan's final point from close to the end-line gave Cavan a second chance.

On a wet October 12, Cavan won the replay. Captain Mick Higgins's free taking that day was second to none. He scored seven of Cavan's nine points and was deservedly nominated 'man of the match', no mean achievement for one who had spent three days in bed with the flu during the previous week! He was voted 'Sports Star of the Week' on October 17 and later on 'Player of the Year'. Mick was described by Jackie Lyne, Kerry ace, as 'the greatest forward I have ever faced bar none'. He was certainly one of the greatest centre half forwards ever. In later years Mick was honoured with Bank of Ireland (1988) and Texaco Hall of Fame (1989) awards.

Seamus Morris's save from a rasper by Meath's captain, Paddy Meegan ('the man in the cap' or was it 'the man with the cap'?) was another memorable feature of the '52 game, which ended with the score Cavan 0-9 Meath 0-5.

It was the first time since 1927 that neither of the All-Ireland teams scored a goal and the lowest score in a final since 1940. Brian Maguire played at centre field for Meath while his brothers Dessie and Liam played at left full back and centre back for Cavan.

The Breffni team on that occasion was as follows: Seamus Morris, Jim Mc Cabe, Phil Brady, Des Maguire, Paddy Carolan, Liam Maguire, Brian O' Reilly, Victor Sherlock, Tom Hardy, Seamus Hetherton, Mick Higgins, Edwin Carolan, J.J. Cassidy, Tony Tighe and Johnny Cusack. Paul Fitzsimons came on for J.J. Cassidy.

Little did we know then (before future stars, Colm O'Rourke or Martin O' Connell, were even born) that Meath's golden years lay ahead while Cavan's were drawing to a close. The men from the Royal County defeated their Breffni neighbours by 1-5 to 0-7 in the All-Ireland semi-final in 1954 before capturing Sam in the final. They would win the All-Ireland in '67, '87, '88, '96 and '99 to bring their grand total to seven but they didn't meet their next door neighbours again in the championship for 51 years. That happened on Sunday July 17 2005 when Cavan got some crumb of long-awaited comfort by defeating them on a score-line of 1-8 to 1-6 in the 3rd round of the All-Ireland Qualifiers!

Cavan won Ulster titles in 1953 and 1954 and had one more glorious championship day when they drew with Kerry (1-13 to 2-10) in the All-Ireland semi-final in 1955. It was my very first time in Croke Park and I watched in dismay from high up in the Cusack stand as that great Kerry wing forward, Tadhg Lyne, punched a goal near the end to earn a draw for the Kingdom. Unfortunately, Cavan suffered a very heavy defeat (4-7 to 0-5) to the eventual All-Ireland winners in the replay. Jim Mc Donnell from Drung, who joined the senior team in 1954, was magnificent on both occasions, particularly in the replay. He curtailed Tadghie Lyne early on and put a stop to John Dowling's 'gallup' when switched to centre-field.

Cavan also gave Down a good run for their money in the 1959/60 National League final only to lose out in the end by 0-12 to 0-9. While they had some wonderful individual performers in the late fifties and early sixties, such as goalkeeper Seamus Morris, Noel O'Reilly, Gabriel Kelly, Tom Maguire, Jim Mc Donnell, Brian Gallagher and his brother Charlie (who was the top Ulster championship marksman in 1964, 1965 and 1967), James Brady and Con Smith to mention but a few, they never re-captured their old team magic or made it to the All-Ireland stage.

For some, 1952 was a year of many 'firsts' – the All-Ireland Fleadh Cheoil was held for the first time, the first car safety belts were manufactured in the U.S.A., the world's first pocket-sized transistor hit the market, the first diesel locomotive came on track in Ireland, Aer Lingus suffered its first fatal accident when the 'St. Kevin' came down in Snowdonia, Emil and Dana Zatopek became the first husband and wife team to win four Olympic gold medals, setting records in all events but for Cavan people the year 1952 stands out for one notable 'last' – 'twas the last year Breffni bonfired Sam!

Cavan, however, did enjoy some moments of glory in the '60's. There was that great occasion in Casement Park, Belfast in '62 when they stopped the Down band-wagon with its star-studded forward line of Paddy Doherty, Sean O'Neill and James Mc Cartin on a score line of 3-6 to 0-5. 40,000 turned up to watch that match. Jimmy Stafford, a former St. Patrick's College full back and Mc Rory Cup star, played out of his skin that day to record a goal in each half. Ray Carolan, a player who would give outstanding service to the county for many years, also caught the eye. They led Roscommon at half-time in the All-Ireland semi-final, thanks to a well taken James Brady goal, but their shooting boots let them down in the second half and despite Jim Mc Donnell saving a penalty (when he stood in for the injured keeper), the Connaught men qualified by two points.

They got the upper hand of the great Down team again in '64, winning by 2-10 to 1-10 at the same venue. Peter Pritchard, another St. Pat's man, scored the second vital goal with his lethal left foot. Later on, they lost to Kerry by 2-12 to 1-7.

They also defeated Down in '67 by 2-12 to 0-8. John Joe O'Reilly and Michael Greenan were the two goal scorers. Many ardent followers thought they would go all the way that year, but sadly they had to succumb to Cork by a single point.

A fourth victory over Down in '69 (the year Gene Cusack, a very talented player, shared the top scoring position in Ulster with Sean Woods of Monaghan) led to a draw against Offaly and a replay defeat (3-8 to 1-10).

The 1970's was a pretty bleak period for Cavan, but at least two players did make it to the record books. Steve Duggan was the top scorer in the Ulster championship in 1976 with a tally of 1-22, while Donal Donohoe made it to the top in 1978 with his 0-12.

A Mc Kenna Cup victory in '88 (following successes in the same competition in '62 and '68) and two great runs to the All-Ireland in the U-21 series in '88 (Offaly 0-11 Cavan 0-9) and '96 (Kerry 1-17 Cavan 2-10) restored some little pride.

However, Cavan's dormant period at senior championship level didn't end until their resurrection under Martin Mc Hugh in '97. They defeated Derry by a single point in the Ulster final and there wasn't a dry Cavan eye in St. Tiernach's Park, Clones when Stephen King raised the Anglo-Celt cup. If Cavan had got the penalty that the great Kerry sports journalist, Con Houlihan, felt they deserved, in their semi-final against his native county that year, who knows but captain Stephen, the Reilly trio (Peter, Larry and Damien), Ronan Carolan (who scored 2-138 for his county), Dermot Mc Cabe and Co. could have gone on to claim Sam. They led at half-time (1-7 to 0-9), thanks to a well-taken goal by Fintan Cahill, but great goalkeeping by Declan O' Sullivan, a brace of points by Maurice O'Sullivan and a goal by Mike Frank Russell sealed Cavan's fate. It was just another 'might have been' - like the one sixty years earlier (1937)

1947 All-Ireland winning Cavan team and officials.

against the same opposition when Pakie Boylan's famous 'winning' point was disallowed in the closing stage of the All-Ireland final. Believe it or not, many people, including wireless commentator, Canon Michael Hamilton, went home that day quite convinced that Cavan had won the match and chalked up their third All-Ireland.

Away back in the halcyon days of the 1940's and '50's, there was more to the football calendar than All Irelands. Before reaching the final stages of the competition, the Breffni men had to deal with their great rivals in Ulster and it was every young lad's wish to accompany his father to the provincial final in St. Tiernach's Park, Clones. Here, from the time that great arena opened in August 1944, there was always a real carnival atmosphere as farmers lay aside their preoccupations with turf and hay to join 'townies' in urging on their county heroes. Some cycled up to fifty miles to witness the event. Hordes, aged from nine to ninety, succumbed to the incessant chant 'Colours of the game, get your colours of the game', and decked in 'hats, scarves and arm-bands' with coats tightly tucked under their oxters, climbed the steep Church Hill and sidled through the narrow passages and turn-stiles. Empty pockets on the Hill and all around the grounds would fill up during the Minor match while there was still lots of friendly banter among the rival fans, in striking contrast to the electric charged atmosphere that would prevail when the adrenalin started to flow during the Senior game and people began to lose 'the run of themselves'.

As the players lined up behind the band to march around the field, we sensed that the real action was about to commence. Then there was the usual passionate rendering of the National Anthem as staunch Gaels from every part of 'Occupied Ulster' savoured their sense of total freedom and comradeship with fellowmen from the South. However, once the referee threw in the ball it was 'dog ate dog' to the final whistle.

I can still remember the pride I felt seeing Phil 'The Gunner' Brady in his royal blue emerge with the ball securely fastened under his left arm and several saffron clad 'lodgers' flowing from his back and sides!

Most games seemed to end with Cavan out in front. Can you envisage the football fever in a county that won five All Irelands and a National League within nineteen years? Can you imagine or can you remember what it was like as a young fellow seeing Sam arrive three times between four and eight years of age. We can put that in perspective by noting the fact that no one in the county under 60 or so today has ever had a chance to relish All-Ireland glory. They have had to sit back and watch former Ulster Gaelic football minnows, Down, equal their county's proud record with glorious All-Ireland victories in 1960, '61, '68, '91 and '94 and Donegal ('92), Derry ('93), Armagh (2002) and Tyrone (2003 and 2005) make their break through, while they themselves suffered the ignominy of so many barren years without Sam. The rot began to set in away back in the late 50's and early '60's when Kevin Mussen and his red and black Mourne brigade began to tear through the Cavan defence and teach the 'old masters' some new tricks.

Swaying over and back in the crowd after the game in Clones, with nothing but shoes and boots below and a speck of sky above, could be a terrifying experience. Such relief when you were hoisted up on an adult shoulder and could watch the throng streaming down the hill, waiting on the railway gates to re-open, or assembling outside the Creighton Hotel hoping to quench their thirsts before boarding the special buses and trains laid on for the day.

If you couldn't make it to the games, our friend Micheál O' Hehir was always there with his live and exciting commentaries. From that Sunday away back in 1938, when as an eighteen year old he covered the All Ireland championship semi-final between Galway and Monaghan in Mullingar, until almost fifty years later, this 'Voice of Gaeldom' became the eyes for thousands of G.A.A. enthusiasts. He knew the games inside out, having travelled to football and hurling matches all over the country with his father, Jim, who had helped to train his native Clare team to All-Ireland hurling success in 1914, was chairman of St. Vincent's and a member of the Dublin County Board. Of course Micheal himself played as a wing-forward for Croke's and St. Vincent's. We couldn't wait to hear his 'Bail O Dhia oraibh go leir, a chairde Gael. Hello everybody and welcome to Croke Park' or on All-Ireland day it was 'welcome wherever you may be'. In 1953, when the final between Kerry and Armagh was first relayed to Africa via Radio

Micheal O' Hehir renewing his friendship with Peter Donohoe, the 'Babe Ruth' of '47.
Photo Courtesy of Cavan County Museum, Ballyjamesduff.

Brazzaville, following a special request from Irish missionaries there, his voice was heard on a ship anchored close to Hong Kong.

Shortly after setting the scene, there was absolute silence all round once he announced, 'the ball is in and the game is on.' We remained glued to the set as he shared his wonder – 'Will he go for a goal or settle for a point?' We too focused on the player almost life-like there in front of us with 'socks down around his ankles, bending, lifting and striking.' As the great Mick O'Dwyer pointed out, 'he could generate unbelievable passion'. We experienced his excitement as he described every puck and kick, every 'schemozzle' in around the square and cried out, 'It's a goal!' These words and many of his other phrases are indelibly etched in the minds of all those lucky enough to have listened to his voice. His sensitivity to the feelings of players and their relations didn't allow him to elaborate on what he called the 'incidents'. On at least one occasion he made the rather telling comment, 'For the life of me, I don't know what that booing is all about'! Whenever he divulged that a player from each side had been sent off, you had to make your own deductions. Sadly, Micheal suffered a debilitating stroke in 1985 and was unable to cover what would have been his 100th All-Ireland final. He was permanently confined to a wheelchair until he died on the 24th. November 1996. Ar dheis Dé go raibh a anam dilis'.

During those impressionable years, we also learned something of the transience of life. We witnessed the sad and untimely deaths of two of Cavan's most famous sons, P.J.Duke, 'the fearless champion from sweet Stradone', and the gallant John Joe o'Reilly. The news of their deaths, like that of twenty-four-year-old Cormac Mc Anallen's in '04, cast a cloud over the entire country and indeed over Gaels everywhere.

P.J. died from pleurisy in St. Vincent's hospital, Dublin on the 1st of May 1950, less than two months after winning a Railway Cup medal with Ulster on St.Patrick's day. He was only twenty five at the time. A dentistry student in U.C.D., he won three Sigerson Cup medals there, playing at centrefield in '45 and '47 and as centre half back in'49. He was captain of the '47 team. He gave a wonderful display of his footballing skills at centrefield and when switched to the half back line in the Polo Grounds, New York that same year. He also 'played his heart out' against Mayo in the '48 All-Ireland.

John Joe, who had led his team mates alongside P.J.'s cortege as it passed along O' Connell Street, Dublin in 1950, died himself just over two years later on the 21st. of November, 1952, at the age of thirty four, while undergoing an operation for a kidney complaint at the Curragh Military hospital. Comdt. John Joe was brought back to his native Killeshandra on a gun carriage, his coffin draped in the tricolour with his officer's cap and sword on top, amid scenes of terrible grief. He had a most illustrious career. During his college days, he captained St. Patrick's College, Cavan, to two Mc Rory Cup victories. He won two County Championships with Cornafean in 1937 and 1938 and also won a Co. Kildare championship medal. He joined the Cavan Senior team in 1937 and was to play in six All Ireland Senior finals. His brother, 'Big Tom' was captain for the first three (in '37,'43 and '45) while he himself captained the other three (in '47, '48 and'49). He won a National Football League medal and four Railway Cup medals with Ulster in '42, '43, '47 and '50 (three of these as captain). He also excelled at basketball and was a notable athlete.

Apart from all this, he was considered one of the finest Gaelic captains of all time. Joe

John Joe O' Reilly leading the Cavan team as the late P.J. Duke's courtage passes along O' Connell Street, Dublin.
Photo of P.J. inset (Photo- Cavan County Museum, Ballyjamesduff)

Keohane of Kerry said that he was 'the greatest leader of men on a playing field' he had ever known. Highly intelligent and always 'fighting fit', he could mark a man and still play the ball. He was good humoured and well recognised as the most popular officer in the Irish army at the time. It came as no surprise when he was listed on the official Football Team of the Millennium. John Joe (1919 – 1952), 'the pride of Cornafean' is commemorated in 'The Gallant John Joe', a song written by the great Swanlinbar patriot, poet and songwriter, Peter Albert Mc Govern. This is regularly sung at Cavan gatherings at home and abroad to this very day.

> *'He led Cavan to victory on a glorious day*
> *In the Polo Grounds final where Kerry gave way,*
> *In Croke Park the next year when our boys bet Mayo*
> *Once again they were led by the gallant John Joe.'*

As noted in the song, 'while the Shannon from Cuilcagh would flow, we'd never have another like the gallant John Joe'. In the G.A.A. centenary year, John Joe and P.J. were selected for the Millennium Year Team chosen by readers of 'The Anglo Celt'. Other players from the 40's and 50' selected included Phil 'The Gunner' Brady (Mullaghoran,), Tony Tighe, Mick Higgins and Peter Donohoe (Mountnugent) and Joe Stafford (Killinkere).

Swanlinbar G.F.C., founded in 1904, was reorganized in 1942. A host of players spring to mind when you think of that decade and the one that followed: Owen Roe Mc Govern, Tommie Gregory Mc Govern, Frs. Paddy and Greg Mc Govern, Bertie Mc Govern, Patsy, Gabriel and Ben Mc Hugh, Joe, Sean and Charlie Young, Christy Creamer, Terry Martin, Tommie and Michael Maguire, Eamon, Frankie and Sean Mc Donnell, Tommie Reilly, Jim Mc Barron, Joe and Packie Maguire, John James Cassidy, Paddy Mc Govern, Pat Mc Manus, Liam and Terry Woods, Benny Mc Kenna, Aidan Felix Mc Govern, Sonny Mc Manus, Hugh Mc Brien, M. Coughlan (Principal,Tiercahan N.S.), Christy Crowe, Phil Mc Brien, James and Joe Mc Govern, Packie and Hugh Prior, Jim Mc Hugh, John Mc Vitty, Tommy Farrelly from Corlough, Enda Maguire, Seamus Reilly, Johnny Mc Govern, Jim Keating (uncle of well known singer, Ronan) and so many others. All gave sterling service.

Sometimes the club went through the doldrums and had to be resuscitated, as was the case in 1952 when Joe Connaughton, Ben Mc Hugh, Fr. Brennan and Johnny Prior got it back on track. It continued to compete right through the 1950's and 1960's and gave a good account of itself considering the fact that at that particular time it could only 'draw' on half the parish and had no permanent sports field. Sometimes it had access to 'Mac's field', on other occasions it had to make do with Gubrawooley or Leonard's field in Uragh. It was often badly depleted through emigration and a small band of dedicated players often had to 'plough a lonely furrow'. The team could generally hold the foe in check for the first ten or fifteen minutes but after that heads began to drop as players came to accept the inevitable. Despite everything, the club kept going, inspired by dedicated workers such as the genial Bob Hughes, a former Manchester policeman, who created something of a record in the late 1960's when the Swads took him to their hearts and elected him chairman.

Swanlinbar eventually made it to the 'upper echelons', winning Cavan Junior League titles in '81 and '84, the coveted Championship in 1985, '98 and 2006 and gained senior status in 1999 thanks to the spirit of the players and the dedication and hard work of Ben Mc Hugh and 'backroom boys', Tony Cullen, Pat Brennan, Oliver Prunty, T.P. Prior, Sean Gilheaney, Michael Leydon, Pierce Mc Barron , John Mc Vitty and Ciaran Mc Govern. I'll leave the full story of their success to another scribe for another time.

2006 saw the opening of the club's redeveloped pitch and refurbished dressing rooms. What a change from those far-off days when players had to tog out in wind and rain under 'The Big Tree' or 'neath the limited shelter of a scrawny river-side bush. Occasionally, they had access to Woods's store (formerly called 'Bridge House'). Then, anointed with goose's seam or that aromatic, semi-medical compound known as 'wintergreen', they went 'clippidy-clop' or 'clackedy-clack' in their leather-cogged boots across the bridge and down past Mc Manus's bicycle shop and 'The Steel' to 'give their all' for Swad!

The Kinawley parish U-14 squad competed very successfully in the Rural Section of the Cavan Schools' League. Playing in this competition for the first time, it defeated Mullaghoran 1-4 to 0-6 in a thrilling game, refereed by Fr. Tom Mallon, St. Patrick's College, in Breffni Park on Sunday evening 22nd July 1956. The Mullaghoran boys were ahead by 0-5 to 1-0 (scored by P.Murphy) but Kinawley, led by their inspirational captain, Frankie Mc Manus and 'the one and only' 'Butty' O'Brien rallied in the second half and Sean Mc Manus's final point gave them victory. The team on that historic day was: T.McDonald, B.Murphy, A.Curry, T.Cullen,

K.Murphy, S.Cullen, G.Owens, F.Mc Manus (Capt.), S.Mc Manus, S.O' Brien, Tony Cullen, J.Mc Hugh and P. Murphy.

Cissie Mac in the 'Swanlinbar News' of 28/7/56 recorded the home coming as follows: 'Crowds carrying torches met the victorious team on the Bawnboy road and the players were borne shoulder-high through the streets. Cheer after cheer rent the midnight air as the cup was proudly displayed. The cup, which is on display in Cullen's drapery business, is attracting large crowds daily.'

It is interesting to note that two brothers on that team of '56 came to public prominence in later years. Sean Mc Manus was ordained and became President of the Capitol Hill-based Irish National Caucus in the U.S.A. while his brother Frankie figured prominently in the Northern Ireland Civil Rights campaign. He became chairman of the Association in Fermanagh, was elected M.P. for Fermanagh/South Tyrone on a nationalist 'Unity' ticket in 1970 and now has a thriving law practice in Lisnaskea and Clones.

The team lost to Mullaghoran in the 1957 decider, but avenged that set back when they defeated their old rivals rather convincingly (4-6 to 1-5) at the semi final stage in 1958. They recaptured the Duke cup that same year by defeating Kill (1-6 to 0-1) in the final played in a wet and slippery Breffni Park. The team included V.Farrell, F.Mc Carthy, M.Maguire, J.Mc Hugh, J.Curry, S.Cullen, A.Cullen, P.Mc Govern, T.P. Prior, N.Smith, J. Mc Manus, E, Mc Govern and P.Mc Hugh.

Schoolboy Champions – The Kinawley team that won the Cavan Schools League Final (Rural section) and Duke Cup by defeating Kill in '58. Front row: V. Farrell, F. Mc Carthy, M. Maguire, J. Mc Hugh, J. Curry, S. Cullen.
Back row: A. Cullen, P. Mc Govern, T.P. Prior, N. Smith, Jim Mc Manus, E. Mc Govern and P. Mc Hugh.
Photo courtesy of the Anglo - Celt

Johnny Prior (driver) and Paddy Leydon (conductor) who gave 70 years cumulative service on the GNR/CIE Cavan-Enniskillen bus route.

In the Cab

In those early years, I shadowed my father whenever and wherever I could
Unfortunately, his time at home was limited. He drove a dark blue and cream G.N.R.and later
a red C.I.E. bus between Cavan and Enniskillen for over forty years.

He either had to leave home at 7.15a.m. in order to ferry employees of the Canadian Taylor
Wood's nylon factory (1949-1966) to work for 8a.m. or else bring others such as the Wellworth
staff and secondary schoolchildren one hour later. He didn't get home until 9.45p.m. on a
Saturday night and was glad to supplement his modest wage by taking pilgrims to Knock or
Pioneers to Bundoran on some summer Sundays. As well as taking control at the wheel, he
was also expected to give his conductors, Frank Mc Govern or Paddy Leyden, a hand to hoist
bicycles and other cargo onto a rack on top of the bus via a step ladder attached to the back.
During the war he had to drive through the North on parking lights with all passenger
windows blanked out so as not to attract the attention of German pilots. At that time buses,
like trains, were overcrowded because private cars were virtually put off the road owing to
the petrol shortage. He witnessed emigrants embark on the first stage of their journey abroad.
They often left with frayed suitcases, Travel Permit Cards, hopes,fears, good wishes and little
else. He enjoyed greeting them on their return, the London 'geezers' clad in their black suits
and fancy ties, the women in 'mod' fashion gear, 'all done up to the 99's, some with
apprehensive-looking partners in tow. Of course there were many who never made it back.

I joined him in the evenings as he reversed his bus 'into bed' in Felix's garage, watched him
plank his cap on the E.S.B. meter and later (as a part-time farmer) clean out the byre and fodder
the cattle. My job was to focus the horizontal beam of the torch on the cow's 'elder' and hold
her tail as he sat on his three-legged stool with a bucket between his knees and made 'the
music of milking'. Soon that sound was muffled in the warm frothy foam. I helped him put the
heavy lock on the gate leading to our hayshed whenever there was a dance in nearby St. Mary's
Hall. I didn't know the purpose of that exercise and what's more, I wasn't told!

On Sunday we often went for a long walk after Benediction and I was delighted to have
him all to myself. When he stopped for 'a few words ' with neighbours, I soon got restless and
tugged impatiently at his coat tail or pocket to encourage him on his way. Sometimes we had
to pass the travelling people, who lived under canvas that was stretched tightly over hazel
rods.

'Putting out' dung, splitting seed potatoes and dusting them with lime, pegging the line for
a new ridge, 'guggering' (dropping the 'split' into a hole), shovelling (or 'moulding') and spraying
the fresh stalks, picking and spreading out onions to dry on the flat roof of the shed, chopping
timber, clipping hedges, foddering the cattle, setting up roosts for the hens or closing them in

for the night, holding the scythe-stone, thinning turnips, cleaning out shoughs (drains) and snowcemming the house were all partnership tasks.

Saving the hay took precedence over everything else and my father was always 'like a hen on a hot griddle' until this work was done. In the 40's, Joe Mc Auley would arrive in from the country and get things under way. Little did he realize as he proudly sat back on his horse-drawn mowing machine, his crooked pipe tucked firmly in the corner of his mouth and slowly and calmly circled our big meadow, that in a very short time the Ferguson would take over, the pace of life would accelerate and within a decade or two there would be many radical changes.

Crows and gulls, on the look-out for frogs, insects, worms and snails, would land on Joe's flat neat swaths and peace would reign for at least a day after his departure but then, if the weather was good, it was a case of 'all hands on deck'. The swaths had to be turned with wooden rakes and later tedded with pitch-forks. Finally the crispy hay was pitched, carried or rolled with a 'Tumbling Paddy' into great circles before being built into rucks or cocks.

Sometimes it wasn't quite as straightforward as that. Our hearts would sink when my father, on seeing the dark, black clouds loom overhead and feeling rain in the air, would announce that we'd have to make 'laps'. This was a monotonous, backbreaking task. My aunt would try to dissuade him from 'going down that road' by assuring him that so long as there was enough blue in the sky to make a pair of pants for a sailor or a cape for the Virgin Mary, there was no need to panic. Someone else might have a story about ridges of high pressure moving in from the Atlantic. Finally, a case might be made to go down a different road and opt for 'hand-shakings' instead. Still, laps it had to be! We 'tucked into' shaking the hay by hand, folded it over the arm and let it sit lightly on the ground so that the wind blew right through it. If you were unlucky you would come across the odd thistle – not a very pleasant fellow – in the process.

When my father was convinced that the hay was dry and in no danger of sweating, we would pitch it in circular fashion around the proposed site and building would commence. I just loved to get up on the newly formed butt of a cock, walk around in circles tramping the hay and packing it down. Of course, the centre needed the odd tramp too in order to bind the whole thing together. When it was time to start heading the cock, I would get orders to 'stay put' and just get the hay under my feet. When headed, I would slide down gently before it was finally raked and hay-roped. Sometimes, if this wasn't done smartly, the wind might come with 'a wild hurroosh' and the whole top would have to be re-done. Then you'd hear someone say 'Bad cess to it anyway' or something that sounded slightly more derogatory! From time to time my mother would arrive with a sweet can of hot tea and some well-buttered scones and you'd swear all your Christmases had come!

Just when you thought the haymaking was over, my father, while driving past in his bus, would notice that a cock or two had 'shifted a bit to the Kildare side'. No more than the potato drills or ridges having to be straight, hay stacks had to stand erect! Otherwise, you'd be the talk of the place and we couldn't have that! So, he wouldn't rest easy until he got off his uniform, released the 'Hairy Ned' or 'home-made' twisted hay ropes ('sugans'), pulled the butt, raked it down and reheaded it with the surplus hay. Lastly, he would top it with fresh grass (the 'greeshoch') cut with the scythe. This he reckoned would take a set and waterproof the whole lot.

My mother, Alice, tending her roses, my father, Johnny, clipping his hedge.

Speaking of the scythe reminds me of another possible haymaking scenario. If the weather was very bad and meadows became waterlogged or if an area was inaccessible to the horses and mowing machine, the grass had to be cut with a scythe. This was a rather complicated instrument that had a long wooden handle that in turn had two short handles attached and a curved blade at the end. It had to be set to suit the height and gait of the particular mower. Sharpening the scythe with a special stone was an art in itself. With all the proper adjustments made and a sharp edge, a good mower could account for three roods a day.

After about three to four weeks when the hay was seasoned, we would hang on to the cocks at the back of the low flat iron-wheeled shifter (which was made from wood and reinforced at the back with a sheet of metal) as Paddy Lunney's or Peter Cassidy's horse drew them back to the haggard or shed . This was the best of crack. First of all, the shifter (or bogey, as it was called in some parts) was reversed under the musty base of the cock. Next, two strong ropes were drawn out and hooked together at the back. Such joy in anticipation as we then listened to the clicking of the hand winches in front lever the cock on board!

Later when the last 'traneen' was trapped, you could sense my father's relief and joy as he surveyed the thatched rick or pikes in the haggard or the full shed of hay. He knew he would have enough fodder for his stock during the long, dark and dreary winter months ahead. Any petition made at this time was sure to get a positive response!

From time to time, he would take me on his 3.30 p.m. bus to Enniskillen. When very young I loved to get into the cab beside him. This was a section cut off completely – apart from a small sliding window – from the rest of the bus. Wellworths, a child's paradise, was generally our first port of call. Here you could get lost in another world with guns, holsters and caps, wooden pencil cases with sliding lids, water pistols, boxes of bubbles, Dinky toys, 'dot to dot' and colouring books, masks, sweets such as 'Spangles' not available in the South.

Across the street there was 'The Melvin'. You went in through a shop run by a Miss Pope from Cloone who, much to my embarrassment, tousled my hair, fidgeted with the collar of my shirt or nipped my neck! She never seemed to tire of marvelling at how big I was getting and wondered how my father could afford to keep me in trousers! Then it was up the stairs to Miss Pope 2's chandelier-lit restaurant for a plate of chips, the like of which I haven't tasted since.

As I moved around with my father in those days, I was very conscious of the great rapport between him and those he met. He could discuss the most recent Gaelic matches with one or listen to another tell how he 'got over the Twelfth'. He really had great friends on both sides of the religious divide.

At that time some shops had a very intricate but interesting system of conducting cash transactions. Your payment was placed in a glass lidded metal box that was then sent whizzing above your head on a network of wires. This was usually retrieved by an oldish lady in a nearby office who returned your change in the same manner. Some of the bigger shops had fine marble counter-tops where shop assistants in white coats with stubby pencils behind their ears took pleasure in stringing up your brown package.

Occasionally, we paid a visit to the barber, who would hoist me up on to a plank placed across the armchair. I certainly found this experience a welcome change from a visit to the dentist. Here all the talk was G.A.A related. In 1959 when Mc Quillan's Fermanagh beat Kerry

Yours truly aged 3, with sisters Etta and Teresa and one year later with 'all in the bag'!

by 1-13 to 2-3 in the All-Ireland Junior Championship final, the place was abuzz with excitement. 'Twas no wonder. The county had been starved of success for years. Many a man was lucky to escape without a cut to the throat when Teddy Henderson, our barber at that time, sharpened his ivory-handled open razor on a shiny strap suspended from a cup-hook, for Teddy seemed more intent on the exploits of the Traceys, the great Mickey Brewster, Sreenan, Clerkin, Devanney and Co. and on game analysis than on the task in hand!

After 4p.m. the streets of the town became crowded with uniformed boys and girls from Mount Lourdes, Portora, St. Michael's, the Collegiate and other schools, all sizing up the talent as they awaited buses that would stream from the old U.T.A. bus depot later in the evening. Some, intimately entwined and oblivious to all around – even the rousing tunes of the Salvation Army and their pleas 'to follow the paths of righteousness and way of the Lord' - kissed, poured forth honeyed words of love or gazed passionately into their sweethearts' eyes!

Time permitting, we sometimes went up to the swings and slide in the Forthill Public Park. Here you could also watch the Mount Lourders in action on their courts, pretend you were playing a saxophone in the great Thomas Plunkett Victorian Bandstand or climb the 108 spiral steps of Cole's Monument and enjoy a fantastic view of the island town, of Lough Erne and its environs. The place itself was beautifully laid out with wooded areas, walks and shrub gardens.

Finally, it was time to go back past the Ulster Farmers' Mart (established by Jimmy Johnston from Armagh in 1950), climb the well-worn concave steps of the old G.N.R. station and await our return journey. This was a most sociable centre with all sorts of people constantly arriving and departing. It was a real hive of activity with its criss-crossed rails, footbridge and signals. I just loved the whole buzz of the place – the screeching of brakes, the sound of engines being shunted into place and hitched to the wagons, passengers scrambling across the platform to get on board, the opening and banging of doors and strapped windows, the whistling, the

Enniskillen station. The first train arrived here in 1859. The last one left on 30 September 1957.

50

Cole's monument Enniskillen. Built in memory of Sir G. Lowry Cole, it took
twelve years to complete and opened in 1857.

waving of flags, the thunderous roll of mail trolleys along the platforms, the crying, laughing, shouting and gesturing of passengers as the great locomotives with fresh fire in their bellies began to hiss white steam and after a succession of jolts, puff their laborious way out of the station en route to exotic places like Dublin, Belfast, Derry, Bundoran or Clones! I envied the train drivers who wielded such power and even the men in the north-side and south-side signal cabins who presided over it all. There always seemed to be a few men in railway uniform hanging around with thumbs hooked in their waist-coats or braces and their backs to the wall. Their exact role in the proceedings wasn't all that obvious. Perhaps, it was these characters who prompted some wit to declare that 'there is a cure in a railwayman's sweat if you could find it'!

Passing the time at the station was never a problem. You could set the arrow to each required letter on the great iron engraving machine, pull the handle and out popped your printed aluminium plate. You could have a go on the 'Penny Arcade Machine'. All you had to do was pull a lever and shoot a heavy, silver ball-bearing into one of the five 'win' slots. Unfortunately, it tended to favour one of the two 'lose' openings! Then there was the huge weighing machine and another that provided notes on your fortune. I was sometimes 'taken' by the big enamel signs, some exhorting the public on what to do, such as 'Drink Bovril' and others specifying what not to do such as 'Please Do Not Spit In The Carriages'. Others had large fingers pointing to the Booking Office and Parcels Office. I loved to run across the timber-tunnelled passenger footbridge and down the steps at the far side, warm myself on a winter's evening at the great coal fire in the Waiting Room or just browse through the comics on the newsagent's stand. Occasionally, you could be particularly lucky and witness the release of large crates of pigeons from one of the platforms. This only happened in July and September. The poor birds created a desperate racket as they soared skywards and then headed for home.

Eventually it was time to board the bus and say – *'Fare thee well, Enniskillen, fare thee well for a while'.*

The Bathing Pool, Bundoran

BEAUTIFUL BUNDORAN

'Beautiful Bundoran, by your silvery sea,
Your golden strand, charms so grand, ever calling me.'

We usually spent about three to five days in Bundoran or else managed a few day trips during the summer using our father's G.N.R. privilege tickets to go on the 9.55a.m. Express from Enniskillen. Few families in our area could afford such luxury at that time and so it was imperative not to 'go on' about your plans. Otherwise, you'd be accused of blowing your trumpet, suffering from delusions of grandeur or generally rising above your station! You could boast all you liked about picking spuds, about the amount of turf you cut or the hay you saved but as for going to the seaside, for a day – yes, but for anything more, that was tantamount to exclusion from any self-respecting group!

We always seemed to get on the train at the last minute and gave a sigh of relief as our mother slung the baggage on to the netted overhead rack. On our way, we were intrigued by the telegraph wires going up and down as we sped along. The scene was not at all unlike that described by Robert Louis Stevenson in his beautiful poem, 'From a Railway Carriage' –

> *'Faster than fairies, faster than witches*
> *Bridges and houses, hedges and ditches,*
> *And charging along like troops in a battle,*
> *All through the meadows the horses and cattle.'*

Some carriages had separate compartments with sliding doors alongside narrow corridors. We loved to run along these and pass through the rickety melodeon-style carriage connections. If the truth were told, our hearts were often in our mouths but this sense of danger only added to our enjoyment. These same hearts soared as we spied the water tower or great revolving wheel in the Amusement Centre even before we reached the seaside town around 11.35!

As soon as we unpacked in Lynch's or 'Star of the Sea', we were down on the beach gazing at the barnacle and cockle shells in the little rock pools, making sand-castles with our tin Mickey Mouse buckets and long wooden handled spades, or building dams that the insensitive, incoming tide would later destroy. Occasionally, we had to watch helplessly as it carried off a sock or prized featherweight beach-ball to the shores of far-away America!

When young, we were thrilled to 'get a go' on the swinging boats or a ride on the donkey that a kind, weather-beaten warrior 'as old as old could be' led across the strand, but later on we longed for the thrill of going out to sea on 'The Duck', a motorised boat on wheels that rode the great breakers but nearly drowned its occupants in the process! All that was before we made the gigantic leap from Open-Air Ceilidhes up the West End and Richard Fitzgerald dance music in St. Patrick's Hall to the ultimate in entertainment, Brendan 'Hucklebuck' Boyer and his Royal Showband in the Astoria.

Sometimes, we went for a walk up the wooden steps from the beach and around Rougey to see the 'Fairy Bridges' and 'Wishing Chair' and look down on Finner Strand, that seemed to stretch out for ever in front of us. My mother used to usher us quickly past the courting couples on the grassy slopes and turn our attention to the well-tanned locals diving fearlessly from boards at different levels across the channel! From the hill overlooking the main beach, there was a magnificent panoramic view of Bundoran. In the background you could see spectacular views of Donegal Bay including Slieve League, Mullaghmore, the Leitrim glens, Ben Bulben and the Dartry range, as well as the West End outdoor pool, carved from the rocks and filled by the Atlantic Ocean. In the foreground over at the amusements you could see children going up and down, round and round on the graceful hobby horses while sparks flew from the tops of the poles attached to the noisy bumping-cars nearby. I can recall the greasy attendants jumping from car to car sorting out the 'pile-ups', the screams of the occupants and the sight of the odd expert showing consummate skill as he casually touched the steering wheel with one hand while the other lay carelessly over the side. You could hear the high pitched siren herald the end of a ride.

Well-endowed women with 'good sensible' swim-costumes emerged from the privacy of 'mobile' bathing boxes that were half-buried in the sand. The 'costumes' could be hired out for a specific fee. If the day was fine and trade brisk, you might have to wait some time for your particular sized garment to come off modesty duty and take it even before it had time to dry out on the line! Less adventurous women, with dresses tucked into their navy blue or pastel

The Prior sisters (Teresa and Etta) on the rocks!

My wife, Margaret Kirke (centre) from Clones, with sister, Jacinta,
and brother Joe on the hobby horses

Stirling Moss and navigator!

coloured knickers, cautiously tested the water or shrieked with embarrassment as an impish 'Flash' photographer captured the moment for posterity! Old countrymen, with the butts of their trousers rolled up, paddled along the shore while the younger generation played ball or just enjoyed themselves in the sand. Further over, a crowd of more advanced swimmers could be seen diving and splashing in the 'Horse-pool' and 'Sixpenny Pool' while Bridie Gallagher passionately extolled Bundoran's 'golden strand and charms so grand'.

Some old Bundoran citizens like to tell the story of the Cavan woman who arrived in the resort for the first time and wanted the benefit of the sea water but was afraid of the waves. She spied one of the 'costume' women carrying back a bucket of water to wash the sand off a client's feet and persuaded her to sell it for half a crown. It wasn't in a Bundoran woman's nature to refuse a bob or two. So, the Breffni woman went off happy to her room in the guest house and immersed her feet for the evening. Later on, as she was returning the bucket, she noticed that the sea was far out. This prompted her to make the rather telling remark, 'Mam, you must have sold a sight of water today!'

Few places in Ireland at that time highlighted the gap that existed between the rich man and 'the ordinary fellow in the street' as did resorts such as Bundoran. Your common 'five eight' had to make do with a modest guesthouse reeking of Mansion polish with linoleum on the floor and oil-cloth on the table, or else settle for a hired caravan. On a day's visit he was delighted to make some tea on a temperamental Primus stove that had to be pricked, methylated and goaded into action or better still, pour it from a flask. He was singing if he could muster a few soggy tomato, salad or banana sandwiches (even if coated with flying sand!) or purchase some fish and chips from the nearest 'Take Away'.

Then there were those who wallowed in their luxury twenty four foot mobile homes or hired out houses for the summer. Others could be seen winding their way up the driveway to the Great Northern or booking into the Central Hotel or Shene House where, in carpet to the knee, they could sip their morning coffee served on silver trays, enjoy a large Havana after evening tea and tuck into dinner at night or sink into posh deck-chairs with sun-shades by day. Accompanied by their caddies, they enjoyed their rounds of golf in the beautiful 18-hole course by the sea.

Bundoran at various times was inundated with Scotch, Northern Ireland and Southern visitors as well as a Company or two of raw F.C.A. recruits from nearby Finner camp and a sprinkling of Lough Derg pilgrims in transit, trying to pass the time until their midnight reprieve.

When it was nearly time to bid adieu to Bundoran, my mother would purchase some carrageen and duilesc while we packed in the traditional rock and souvenirs, which she would refer to as 'oul junk and trumpery to fill up the house.' Rather than 'burn a hole in my pocket' and hoping against hope that I would finally hit the elusive jack-pot, I would have one final go on the slot machines, nip into 'The Palace of Horrors' or get a last cone in the 'Shell House' before calling it a day.

Monica Kyne (Sunnybank Terrace), Mary ('Charlie') Mc Govern and Josie Gilleece
(Springtown) enjoying Bundoran's bracing breeze and planning the next move!
Photo: Etta Graham

Bob Hughes, his daughter, Colette, Mary Josephine (Molly) Woods and Patsy
Hughes relaxing on the strand. (Photo: Patsy Hughes)

The Beano - circa 1959

Image © DC Thomspon & Co. Ltd.

HOBIES AND PASTIMES

From once you were knee-high in the country, you were expected to do your bit on the farm. Here it was a case of 'all hands on deck'. The days of swinging on the yard gates 'gawking' at those 'going the road' and running back to hide in a mother's skirt didn't last long. On the other hand, most villagers only partook in farming activities on a part-time basis and so their youngsters could devote more time to leisure pursuits. The vast majority of these were outdoor-based. There was no television to entice you inside and besides, adults just ordered you out into 'God's good fresh air' and that was that!

We seldom had a problem finding something to do. Occasionally, we may have been bored 'out of our tree' and just kicked the odd tin along the footpath or mischievously banged Maggie Alec's door and then ran off, or tied a thread to her knocker and watched her reaction from afar. Some of the 'good boys' of Swad were not beyond raiding an orchard, putting a hen to sleep, 'duling' a fish, snaring a rabbit or riding bare-backed on some unfortunate donkey.

However, growing up in the Golden Age of Cavan football, Gaelic was always high on our agenda. Mick Higgins, Tony Tighe, Peter Donohoe, John Joe O' Reilly etc. graced 'Mac's Field' most evenings to repeat their heroic exploits in the company of men such as John Dowling, Jimmy Murray , Jack Mangan or Sean Flanagan. Needless to say, arguments arose as to 'who would be who'. There was often a Micheál O'Hehir on hand behind the goals to provide a full commentary on the match. If we hadn't a sufficient number to form two teams, we'd settle for a game of 'Backs and Forwards'. The football we had back then was laced and made of heavy leather with a rubber bladder inside. It was fine in good weather but if it got wet, you'd be as well off trying to kick a cannonball. If you got a crack of it on the head or worse still, in a more fragile nether region, you'd know the difference. On occasions when there was 'nothing doing' in Mac's field, we'd set down our jerseys as goal posts in the Fair Green or along the road and opt for soccer instead.

The '47-'52 period saw Irish rugby flourish. In 1948 the national team won the coveted Triple Crown and Grand Slam, thus bridging a 49 year gap. Karl Mullen, Jackie Kyle and later, the great Tony O' Reilly, become household names in rugby areas, but the game had little or no impact on us as there were no televisions to whet our appetite and no rugby tradition in most parts of rural Ireland at that time – thanks to some extent at least to the G.A.A. ban on 'foreign' games. The fact that the rugby team's success more or less coincided with that of the Cavan team would have been another important factor. The same was true of soccer at the highest level. The news that Jackie Carey (1919-1995) became the first Irishman to captain F.A. Cup winners when Manchester United defeated Blackpool in 1948, or that the Republic of Ireland (with goals from Con Martin and Peter Farrell) defeated England 2-0 in Goodison Park in September '49 barely registered with people in our area at that time. Shamrock Rover's great success in the '50's, winning the League in '54, '57 and '59 and the Cup in '55 and '56 certainly went unnoticed. I would also have been oblivious to it all if I hadn't heard the Dublin Customs men listening to Philip Green's commentaries on my aunt's wireless. We had the odd 'go' at cricket and hurling but neither really 'caught on.' After the Melbourne Olympics in 1956, we all wanted to run like Ronnie Delaney. Cowboys and Indians were always popular, especially after Santa had supplied the cowboy hats, guns, holsters and caps, or Red Indian outfits with their head bands of coloured feathers as well as the bows and arrows but in the late 50's daring I.R.A. raids also influenced boyhood play.

While St. Mary's Hall was being built, we had no trouble finding long planks and tar barrels. These we used for making see-saws. Despite the warning notices, the skeletal structure of the place also offered endless possibilities for sporting activities. When we got tired there, we'd call in to see what was going on close by in 'Big Mick's' garage. Hugh Joe Gorman 'gave out' the petrol there and on one occasion got a brand new Esso boiler suit with tiger motif. We all envied him and wanted to become petrol attendants when we grew up!

The fishing season began on 1st March and ended at the beginning of October. Whenever there was a 'middlin' flood in the Claddagh, we'd get out our hazel fishing rods with brown line rolled around the tops and black penny eye-hooks attached, dig a good jar of blackheads, head down Felix's lane and pass Young's Fort Hill on our way to the river bank for the evening. Alternatively, after a very heavy downpour, we might head up the mountain and fish down from the Tullydermot Falls. With any kind of luck we'd return with a fine gad (a forked stick) of trout for our tea.

If the fish were not in great nibbling form, we would set our rods in 'Pollawaddy' or 'The Captain's Hole' and then wrestle on the bank, play a very primitive game of cricket, throw burrs at one another or skim stones. We might even exchange 'dirty' rhymes or stories. Apart from the knowledge gleaned while watching sheep, asses and dogs mating or Breen's great white-headed Hereford bull rising to the occasion, this was the only form of sex education available since the time we played 'I'll show you mine if you show me yours'. Like Lewis Carroll's Alice, we were becoming 'curiouser and curiouser' by the day and soon dismissed out of hand the yarns about the stork, the cabbage leaf and the gooseberry bush. We certainly knew that we weren't made from 'slugs and snails and puppy-dogs' tails'. This marked the end of innocence and left us with 'more in our heads than the comb would take out'.

On a very bright summer's day when the fish had a clear view of our intent, we'd try to fool them by going upstream and tramping in bits of the bank and adding a jar or two of worms so that they would think a fresh flood was on its way. This was what we called 'putting down a muddy'. Like Izaac Walton, we knew you had to get inside the mind of the trout. We were absolutely convinced that our scheme had the desired effect but to this day I'm not sure if any subsequent catch was due to our ingenuity or merely coincidental. However, in those childhood days it helped to convince me that 'where there's a will, there's a way', and that was not such a bad lesson to learn early in life.

We never really thought about food along the river bank but once we got home we'd eat the legs off the table. Then our own catch was like manna from Heaven.

Lunney's Ford. Situated in Drumconra (or Low Forge), it was a river crossing point for centuries. It connected the old road to Belturbet, through Gortoral, with the old road to Enniskillen. With its base of flat, neatly cut stone, mini waterfall and irregular stepping stones, it was a place with special allure, especially when water was at a low level. You could paddle, catch 'stridildies'(minnows) or tadpoles in a toy net, skim stones or help 'Big Mick's' men wash the cars there. The dark shells or 'sliggins' of the tiny fish that lived in the gravel beds of the river beside the ford, used to appear 'out of the blue' every summer. We were attracted by their bright 'Mother of Pearl' inner sides shining in the water. Only later did we realize that these belonged to the freshwater pearl mussel known as Margaritigeria margaritiferia.

The Farmer's Hole. Like Brackley Lake, it was a popular bathing spot in the 1940's and 50's - Swad's answer to Bundoran!

The River Blakwater joins the River Claddagh beside 'The Iron Bridge'.

The Iron Bridge was built around 1890 and replaced the stepping stones, which locals used as a 'short-cut' from the Gortoral road to Mass and shopping in the village.

At that time girls liked to skip and play games such as ' Hop-Scotch', 'Donkey', 'Statues', 'Tip Tag',' Hide and Seek', 'Blind Man's Buff' and'Queenie O. Juggling balls and reciting rhymes such as the following at the same time were also popular:

> *Teddy bear, Teddy bear, tip the ground,*
> *Teddy bear, Teddy bear, twirl around,*
> *Teddy bear, Teddy bear, show your shoe*
> *Teddy bear, Teddy bear that will do*
> *Teddy bear, Teddy bear, go up the stairs,*
> *Teddy bear, Teddy bear, say your prayers.*
> *Teddy bear, Teddy bear, put out the light,*
> *Teddy bear, Teddy bear, say good night.*

There was another that started with 'Plainy, clappy, rolley, to-back.' Sometimes they would form a circle and recite that 'Black Death' rhyme :

> *Ring-a-ring-a-rosie,*
> *A pocket- full of posies.*
> *Atishoo, atishoo,*
> *We all fall down'.*

Then there was the one about Paddy on the railway:

> *Paddy on the Railway*
> *Picking up stones,*
> *Up came an engine,*
> *And broke Paddy's bones.*
> *Ah, says Paddy*
> *That's not fair.*
> *Ah, says the engine'*
> *I don't care.*

I'm sure everyone can remember the one about school:

> *Friday night is my delight,*
> *And so is Saturday morning.*
> *But Sunday night, I get a fright*
> *When I think of Monday morning!*

And the call on Janey Mac:

> *Janey Mac, me shirt is black,*
> *What will I do for Sunday?*
> *Go to bed and bury your head*
> *And don't get up till Monday!*

There was also the commentary on the days of the week:-

> *Monday for health,*
> *Tuesday for wealth,*
> *Wednesday the best day of all.*
> *Thursday for losses,*
> *Friday for crosses,*
> *And Saturday no day at all!*

A favourite night-time rhyme went something like this-

> *Night night, sleep tight and don't let the fleas bite,*
> *But if they bite, squeeze them tight,*
> *Then they won't bite 'till to morrow night.*

There were also 'Test your Wits' games such as the following:

> *Supposing, supposing*
> *3 men were frozen,*
> *2 died,*
> *How many were left?*
> *'One'*
> *No, None,*
> *'Cause you're only supposing!*

 Or

> *What is under the fire, over the fire and never touches the fire?*
> *Answer: A cake of bread in a pot oven.*

Girls also spent a lot of their time playing mother, house, shop, hospital and school. Like ourselves, they had to rely more on fantasy and make believe to amuse themselves than children today. Looking after their different dolls, some rag and others with china or delph heads, was a huge commitment. They had to be changed and taken for long walks! Some kept autograph books and collected different things such as stamps. In Summer time, they made daisy chains to wear as necklaces or just lay on the ground holding buttercups under their chins or swung their pony-tails and admired their dresses, new ankle-length bobby socks and brown floral patterned Clark's sandals or simply nattered away. Such a change in 1958 when the hoola-hoop craze hit the world. Then they too were up and at it.

Mrs.Coffey from Clones and Maida Murphy from Kinawley conducted dancing lessons in St. Mary's Hall. With backs straight and hands down by the side, we were doing jigs, reels and hornpipes before we knew where we were. Unfortunately, as time went by, many of us 'mitched' and opted instead for Mac's field. We just weren't destined to become 'Lords of the Dance'!

In the pre-television days especially, we really enjoyed going to the 'pictures' in Woods's Hall once a week. Here a very cross Ballinamore lady wielding a bicycle lamp kept 'smacht' on us as we sat on our forms watching Red Indians and stage-coaches, Davy Crockett, 'King of the Wild Frontier', Hopalong Cassidy and his horse Topper, the Cisco Kid and Diablo, Robin Hood, Friar Tuck and Co., Scotland Yard, Laurel and Hardy and 'The Three Stooges'. There were other memorables such as 'Shane' (1953), 'Seven Brides for Seven Brothers' (1954), 'The Dam Busters' (1955) and 'A Night to Remember' (1958). A false move or squeak and she was on to you right away with her ultimatum, 'one more word and you're out!'

Still, we depended more on books and comics to transport us from our mundane surroundings to the more exciting world of the imagination. When very young, we used to enjoy Count Curly Wee and Gussie Goose, strip cartoons included in the 'Irish Independent'. The text, which was in rhyming couplets, told us of the adventures of the animals in Fur-and-Feather land. At the week-end you had 'Blondie' in 'The Sunday Press' and 'The Phantom' in 'The Sunday Independent'. As we got older we progressed to 'Our Boys', 'Ireland's Own' (with all its ghost stories) and of course, Enid Blyton's Secret Seven (Janet, Peter, Jack, Barbara, Colin, George and Scamper, the dog) whom we accompanied in spirit as they met at the beginning of their holidays in a shed at the bottom of the garden, made their plans and set out on their mystery-solving adventures. They really captivated us with their talk of midnight feasts, of secret tunnels and hiding places, of old ruined cottages, weird noises and ghostly lights. Her Famous Five were no less popular as were G.A. Hendry's books and Captain W.E. Johns' 'Biggles' on the flying exploits of the wartime pilot.

However, for really light reading it was hard to beat a good comic, especially if you only had a short time to spare. There was no shortage of these – the 'Lion' and 'Eagle.'(1950), 'Knockout' and 'Topper' (1953) , 'Hotspur', 'Wizard', 'Tiger', 'Robin' and 'Swift'(1954), 'Roy of the Rovers' & 'Beezer' (1956), 'Rocket' (edited by World War 2 pilot, Douglas Bader) etc. but the 'Beano', first published by D.C. Thompson in 1938, and the 'Dandy' were the most popular in our area. In fact, they were very popular 'all over'. In the mid '50's their combined circulation was over two million copies per week. They were priced at 2d. The Dandy came out on a Tuesday, the Beano on a Thursday. We swapped them around and didn't mind their date or dog-eared condition.

CHARLIE the CHIMP

Who could forget Charlie the Chimp!
Image © DC Thomspon & Co. Ltd.

How could one forget Desperate Dan, The Smasher, Korky the Cat and the newer characters introduced in the 50" such as Dennis the Menace (1951), Rodger the Dodger, The Bash Street Kids, Minnie the Minx and Little Plum! Tin Lizzie gave her name to the famous rock group while many a student in our boys' boarding schools got his nick-name from such notables as Charlie the Chimp, Biffo the Bear, Shaggy Doggy, Hungry Horace, Angel Face or Lord Snooty (with his top hat and Eton collar). I'm sure girls were too sensitive to christen their mates Pansy Potter, Jenny Penny or Cocky Sue! They had their own special comics such as 'School Friend' (1950), 'Girl' (1951), 'Bunty' (1958) and Judy..

I was delighted to discover recently that the 'Beano', which hasn't changed all that much since our day is going strong with a respectable readership of 350,000.It still comes out every Thursday but costs 85cents (around 37 times the price of the 1950 edition!). It now has a website address, *www.beano.com* and several new characters such as Gnasher and Gnipper, Hugh Dunnit, Denis's little sister, Bea, the Mini Menace, Ivy the Terrible, Cuddles, Dimples and Billy Whizz. You can become a Beano Club Member or vote for your Comic Idol. It's comforting to know that the Bash Street Kids, Little Plum, the ingenious Rodger the Dodger and Minnie the Minx have maintained their youth and are not suffering from any infirmity of mind or body! I just wonder what eventually happened to Lord Snooty and the Gasworks Gang.

As my father was a bus driver and carried the various newspapers and magazines, he was given complimentary copies of these for his trouble and so we were never short of reading material. This included 'The Irish Press, 'The Irish Independent', 'The Irish News', 'The Impartial Reporter', 'The Fermanagh Herald' and of course the Cavan man's bible itself, 'The Anglo Celt', first issued on 6th.of February 1846. It arrived every Friday with comprehensive coverage of local and national news and items entitled 'Woman's Work', 'Farm and Garden', 'Sport', 'Diocesan Changes', 'Wit and Humour', 'Power of Prayer', 'Fairs for the week', 'Poultry lectures' and 'LDF Notices'. It even had a 'Poet's Corner' for the more literary minded.

Biffo the Bear and Korky the Cat.
Image © DC Thomspon & Co. Ltd.

The New Bridge and River Claddagh

Like the 'Fermanagh Herald' it let people know what was on offer by way of entertainment with its adverts relating to Pioneer, Parochial, Pancake and Mistletoe dances, Ceilidhe and Old Time, Staff dances (Ladies 10 shillings, Gents 12/ 6, Doubles £1.1s), Variety concerts and plays, Whist and '25' Card Drives, ploughing matches, Hunt Balls, monster bazaars (with their Rickety and Roulette wheels, Rings, Crown and Anchor) etc. A lot of the other adverts were quite health orientated giving the impression that we were a nation of hypochondriacs. There was Zam-Buk for aching feet, Vick for bronchial colds, Embex for flu and headaches, Sloans for Sciatica ('Where's the pain, here's the Sloans'), Silbe for asthma , Jessels tablets to restore strength and health and California Syrup of Figs ('a child's best laxative'). Mutesco was there to keep hair young, Checks was ready to do battle with hoarseness ('Hoarse? Not me. I suck Cheks') and Rennies had the answer to any form of stomach trouble, while the risk of 'catching cold' could b e lessened with Angier's Emulsion. If you weren't keeping 'radiant, youthful and attractively slim', it was time to opt for your quota of Bile Beans or some facial treatment with Pond's Cream ('still your passport to beauty'). Clarke's 'Blood Mixture', Vick's ' Vapour Rub' and Smoker's 'Fur' were also included.

Even the birds and animals were 'covered'! Kossolian was the poultry 'pick me up' to make hens lay and poultry pay. There was 'Cure Ox' for scour, 'Red Drench', ('the supreme remedy for indigestion, loss of cud, red water and dry murrain) and 'Curud' for udder ills. If you were having trouble with crows, 'Kro-No-More' was your man! There were of course some advertisements for more ordinary items such as those for Globo and Pak coffee and Sandeman port. You were reminded to collect your Sweet Afton coupons and get a few 'freebies' e.g. a powder puff for only 170 coupons, a dressed doll for 430. If you didn't wish to get caught with your trousers down, you could pick up braces for 220!

The item 'Swad News' with the personal comments of our local correspondent was relished by all. It covered a wide variety of topics such as accidents, births, marriages, deaths and condolences, court cases, teacher appointments, pilgrimages to Lough Derg and Knock, outings to Bundoran, land sales, fairs and cattle prices, progress on the farm, grouse shooting, visitors, turf stealing, milk scarcity, the first sound of the cuckoo and church ceremonies. Any little bit of sensational news got special treatment. Take the following item that appeared in April 1944 for example. 'A man, horse and cart went over a 50 foot cliff at Gortacashel, Swanlinbar, known locally as 'The Folly Rock'. Mr. James Mc Govern, Mill Street, was unloading manure when he and his horse and cart slipped over the cliff. He managed to jump off into a clump of bushes and the horse and cart finally came to a halt in whitethorn bushes within yards of the flooded Blackwater River. None were any the worse of their experience.'

If there was nothing of note to report, the local correspondent, adept at improvising, had no qualms about spicing things up with the odd fictional item! In January '47 she focused on the arrival of the first paraffin since October '46, which was very much appreciated by many who had spent Christmas in semi-darkness. We were told that Jaffa oranges in windows gave the shops a pre-war appearance, while an unfortunate publican had a fine of one shilling imposed for keeping open until 10.10p.m. He explained that his clock was ten minutes slow.

The 'Celt', like other newspapers at that time was almost devoid of photographs, certainly by to day's standards, while the headings and general layout were not particularly eye-catching, to say the least.

Apart from getting involved in all these hobbies and interests, there still seemed to be time to 'stand and stare'. We often leaned over the 'New Bridge' (built in 1938), watched the odd salmon struggle to make his way upstream, or just 'whiled away' the time dropping in pebbles and admiring the newly-formed circles or else engaged in peaceful reverie.

When we look back, the good times tend to come to the fore but naturally enough, there were occasions when things were not quite 'hunky-dory'. First and foremost there was a host of varied creatures from another world who constantly kept tabs on us. There was the threat of the 'Bogey Man', that evil or mischievous spirit who lurked around every corner watching out for a boy who did not eat up his dinner or do what he was told! There were fairies, supernatural beings usually represented in diminutive human form, who played around lone blackthorn bushes, had magical powers and could whisk you off to some far-away region. No boy in gansey and short pants, however brave or adventurous, wanted to join those already 'gone with the fairies'. Of course, the devil and his cohorts, who resided in Hell, presented a far greater threat. What if they arrived on the scene complete with horns and hoofs to carry you down below? That would be the scenario if you committed a mortal sin or made a bad confession. As if we hadn't enough to contend with, you also had ghosts, the disembodied spirits of dead people. These went about their business in pale shadowy form and liked to haunt the living. They were supposed to be pretty common during the winter months, especially around Halloween or in the month of November. The Banshee belonged to this category and her wail was supposed to herald the imminent departure of some poor soul.

Apart from the supernatural, there were also some earthly worries. Minor misdemeanours or transgressions could spark the threat of a night in the 'clink' or 'black hole' of a Garda barracks. Even if based locally, it did present a terrifying prospect for any young lad still in short corduroy pants! So too did the idea of being chased by a bull or gander. Being forced to take potions of castor oil, cod liver oil, Milk of Magnesia or Syrup of Figs, or having to bed down with those who already got the measles so that 'we'd get the whole thing over at once' wasn't much 'craic'. Suffering the pain of a hot poultice, having to go up the Tanyard Lane to the old Dispensary (formerly the tannery) for an injection or tooth extraction and listening to Nurse 'Barney' telling you not to be a sausage, carrying arm-wrecking buckets of drinking water from the Steel Well or from the pump in the Canon's back yard, getting a sting from a bee, wasp, or nettle or accidentally sitting on a hill of 'pismires' (ants) also took some of the gloss off living.

Occasionally a sudden death or local tragedy would cast a dark cloud over the entire village and leave a deep impression. One night there was a terrible crash that claimed the life of a very talented young man in his prime and injured the other occupants. Next morning we shuddered at the sight of congealed blood on the crumbled wreck. Sometimes we would hear whisperings about the murder of a beautiful 19 year old girl on an isolated boreen at Gortoral near Lunney's ford. Even though this had happened away back in 1923, murder at that time was such a rare occurrence, it was still referred to in hushed tones. Several other villagers died tragically at home and abroad, and we all felt deep sympathy for 'Big Mick' Mc Govern and Hubie Dolan when their premises went on fire.

Another abiding fear was that the communist Soviets would 'bate the Hell' out of the Yanks, take over the entire world and wreck our freedom in the process. They did seem to be quite a formidable bunch, winning hands down in the Space Race and having 4,000,000 under arms in Eastern Europe. They were so secretive, we never quite knew what they were up to but when, for example, they rolled their tanks into Budapest in 1956 to crush the Hungarian revolution, built the Berlin Wall in '61 or annually displayed their military might in Red Square, they sent a cold shiver down all our little Western spines. We learned that as far back as 1917 Our Lady had exhorted three young Portuguese children at Fatima to pray for the conversion of Russia. This didn't do anything to allay our fears. In fact my sister's teacher used to make capital of these very fears, telling the girls whenever they misbehaved, that the communists would come in the night and cut off their toes! For years afterwards, my sister could only go to sleep curled up like a young pup with her feet a safe distance from the side or bottom of the bed, well away from any prowling, knife-wielding Soviet sadist!

Between this and not being able to cross their legs in case it would make Our Lady blush, the poor girls were doubly handicapped! Later, a further restriction was imposed when some nuns encouraged them to leave space for the Holy Ghost between themselves and their boyfriends!

There were other more home-grown fears – that my father would peel or even slit open his Adam's apple while he shaved with his 'cut throat', or that the styptic pencil or the bits of newspaper he stuck on would not staunch the blood, that my mates would see my visiting American cousin hugging me and planting wet kisses on my cheek, that I would never grow again after walking under Terry Greene's ladder, that I'd have seven years of bad luck for breaking my aunt's mirror and so on.

Still, these fears were transient in nature and quite peripheral. Despite them all, you could say we had 'the life of Riley'! How we enjoyed hearing about the sun dancing on Easter Sunday morning, Santa coming down the chimney, the arrival of the stork or tooth fairy, the flight of the swallow, the life cycle of the delicate butterfly, the busy bee, the leaping salmon, the clever wren with her 'in and out' nest, fast movements and whirring flight, the coal-black blackbird with her bright orange bill and eye-ring and her melodious song, and of course that great harbinger of spring, the mean cuckoo. There was the smell of the lilac in June, of recently mown grass, of the hawthorn and the honeysuckle, of freshly baked white soda, wheaten or treacle bread, of blackcurrant or blackberry jam, not to mention the homely whiff of the turf or ash log at Christmas, the taste of hot tea in the bog or hayfield on a summer's day , of salty scallion sandwiches to be washed down with milk still warm from the cow , of toast made on a fork before the open fire, of a delicious 'guggie' (a boiled free-range egg chopped up with butter while still hot and served in a cup), the sense of triumph on discovering the secret nesting place of a reclusive Rhode Island Red whenever she 'gave the game away' with her loud and proud cackle, the thrill of crouching between the potato ridges during a game of 'Hide and Seek', the simple joys of seeing a cow's apparent smile as she shook her head, swished her tail and chewed a wisp on a winter's night, of a newly born calf learning to stand on her long wobbly legs, or a young 'suck' down on his front knees with bucket on his head, or the skeletal open-mouthed 'scaldies' (young birds) in their nests anticipating their mother's return. Then there were those special dignitaries like Puss 'n Boots, Donald Duck, Mickey Mouse, Brer Rabbit and Gussie Goose. Without realizing it, I came to appreciate the love of God and the beauty of His world manifested at every turn, as well as the joy of community living.

Lizzie Reilly, Carmel Sweeney, Vera Mc Govern and
Mary McGovern with Lizzie's nephews, Peter and
Sean (Owney) Mc Govern. (1948)
Photo: Mary Gallagher (nee McGovern)

UP THE STREET

'The townsman lives in a world that is full of such a number of things that he is bound to pass most of them with his eyes, to all intents and purposes, shut. In a smaller world the human being observes and remembers, to put it mildly, everything. If he seldom travels beyond his own tiny village, he remembers the names of every shop, the position of every house and tree. He knows his village as a child knows its nursery.' Robert Lynd (1879 – 1949)

Looking back, it seems as if we spent a good deal of our time 'only going up the street'. 'Only' belies the significance of these social expeditions that made us so familiar with every footpath, every pole, every hump and hollow, every leaking gutter, peering eye, fading 'Hopscotch' line, shattered Bangor slate on the pavement or Gold Flake package clogging a water gulley, every cracked pane. Above all else, these sorties, at one time or another, brought us face to face with every trader and character about the place. As children, we really had great freedom to move around at will. Neighbours looked out for neighbours' children – there was a kind of communal parenting in vogue –and so our own parents had less need to be concerned about our safety and whereabouts than might be the case to day.

It's quite amazing to think there were 13 pubs in our small village at a time when money was supposed to be scarce. These included Felix J. Mc Govern's 'First and Last', Pee Cassidy's, Hackett's, Hugh Cullen's, Hubie Dolan's, Clarke's, Kilkenny's, Breen's, Mc Steen's Commercial / Peter Drumm's, Annie Owens's / Flanagan's, Sean Young's, Mc Caffrey's and Lunney's. I suppose some thought 13 was a lucky number, others might not have agreed. At that time, those of us in short pants were not yet in a position to judge.

Katie Byrne hadn't a bad bone in her body but she was quaint. In her premises or should I say, Curiosity Shop, alongside Woods's brae, she literally sold everything from a needle to an anchor. A kind of folklore grew up around herself and her brother, Tommie. He liked to be addressed as 'Mr. Byrne'. If you forgot yourself and called him by his christian name, he was known to retort, 'I didn't know we were in the same class'. Katie was reputed to have bought from every single traveller who crossed her threshold and indeed her store bore testimony to this. Every crevice in her house was supposed to be filled with coins and every inch between her rafters was insulated with £5 notes! A creature of the dark, she preferred to snooze by day and stay awake into the early hours of the morning.

When you knocked for attention, you seldom got an immediate response. Just as you were beginning to cope with the unique feline fragrance of the place or about to depart, a pair of piercing beady eyes, set back in a dark skeletal visage beneath a mop of ragged tresses would suddenly appear from behind pitch-forks, axes, picks, rakes, scythes, shears, yard brushes, rolls of 'Hairy Ned' and netting wire, rat-cages, mouse- traps, hay-knives, brush handles, billhooks, sickles, shillelaghs, pulleys and wrenches, Sacred Heart lamps, leprechauns and stacked boxes of hob- nails and horse-shoes, and a hoarse, monotonous voice would break the eerie silence with a rather half-hearted query, 'Well, boy, what can I do for you?.' Soon she would lay her gnarled bony fingers on the desired item, take your cash, fumble about in the till and limp off through the clutter without any further ado. Shortly after she died in 1973, people came from far and wide to her long-running auction, which was conducted by well-known Bundoran

Main Street Swanlinbar. John and Mickey Reilly's single storey house at the entrance to the Tanyard Lane – the last thatched house in Swad – can be seen on the right. It was destroyed by a Loyalist bomb on September 21st 1974. Earlier in July that year a bomb damaged the 'First & Last' premises of highly respected 87 year old publican, Felix J. Mc Govern. It also damaged Terry Greene's next door. On December 8th, also in that ill-fated year, St. Mary's Church, which had been built in 1829, reconstructed in 1959 and renovated the previous year, was completely destroyed.

auctioneer, Sean Meehan. For years afterwards, you would hear people say, 'I got that at Katie Byrne's auction'.

I also enjoyed a visit to Prior's where Pat, the proprietor, a former St. Aidan's Templeport star, would lean across the counter and wax lyrical 'till the cows came home' about the feats of great Cavan teams and the county's future prospects. How proud he would have been if he had lived to see his grandson, Thomas, wear the Breffni No.3 jersey. Sometimes, Andy Kelly, the village's G.A.A. historian, might enter and, for devilment or otherwise, set some argument alight! Pat's daughter, Kathleen, gave a big 'Tuppenny', 'Thrupenny' or 'Sixpenny' (a quarter of a block of ice-cream between two wafers), as did Kathleen Kilkenny, and so they got plenty of young customers during the lazy, hazy days of summer.

Then there was Joe Smith's where you could sit on a form, eat biscuits or Tayto crisps, wash them down with fizzy Club Orange (a 'designer' drink in the early '50's!) or Nash's Red Lemonade, and remain on having the 'craic' long after your money ran out. There were also times when we engaged in some heated arguments there with Fermanagh supporters of the great Down teams!

Mrs. Lena Mc Goldrick kept a tobacco and confectionery-cum-second-hand clothes shop. She also had a small lending library on the side. I was often dispatched to collect some book by Annie M. P. Smithson, Agatha Christie, Sir Arthur Conan Doyle or Canon Sheehan for my mother. She would add on the way out, 'Mrs. Mc Goldrick will know what I have read or what

Big Mick Pat Jack Mc Govern's and the Spa House with Mick's taxis parked outside.
Inset, Big Mick.
Photo: Mary Gallagher (nee McGovern)

would be of interest to me'! That's just the way things were then. Around Christmas time Mc Goldrick's specialized in a completely different line. It became a toy shop. Then we would spend ages peering into their large display window. As I look back now, toys and decorations from the post-war years and '50's parade before my eyes in a unique assembly – Meccano and Bayco sets, a 'Jack-in-the-Box', Chinese Chequers, Tiddly Winks, Snakes and Ladders and Ludo games, sets of water colours, the Mr. Potato Head Funny Face kits, soldiers, 'melojins', bugles, tin whistles and Hohner mouth-organs, whipping and musical spinning tops, yo-yos, guns and holsters, mingled with necklaces, rag dolls, gollywogs, nurses' outfits, cups and saucer, post office and beauty sets, skipping ropes with wooden handles and such stuff for the girls. Coloured lights, Christmas stockings, berried holly, shreds of tinsel and the odd large bell-shaped decoration, all with a light touch of snow completed the picture of a winter wonderland. What a change on Christmas morning when there was nothing on view but the heads of thumb tacks and crepe paper. It never occurred to us, as local Customs officers gave a detailed account of Santa and his reindeers passing the border post, that Mrs. Lena Mc Goldrick was the one who helped the old man fill his sacks on Christmas Eve!

Mrs. Ellen Reilly, a warm, motherly figure with wrap-around apron, catered for anyone with a sweet tooth. Known to many as Ma Reilly, she always had a steady stream of young customers. Peggy's leg, lucky bags, fizzy bags, Gobstoppers, Dolly mixture, Conversation lozenges, cough mixture sweets, Cleeves slab-toffee and boiled sweets that came in a can,

Ben McHugh

Tommy Gregory McGovern

white Clarnico Murray sweets, bars of Urney Regal chocolate, ropes of liquorice, sherbet, Refreshers, Long John bubble gum, Superhero and golf ball chewing gum, a Golly bar, Dime, Wham and Macaroon bars, every kind of trash! You name it. She had it. Even if you didn't know exactly what you wanted, you could ask, 'What can I get for a penny or a thrupenny bit?' and she would always send you off happy with a lock of nice sweets. Come to think of it, so many of the very important things in life at that time could be bought for a penny – a bar of toffee, jelly babies, aniseed balls, gobstoppers, an ice lolly or ordinary lolly, a marble thaw, a pencil, a writing nib, a fishing hook, even a copy of the Catechism! What's more, with that princely sum, depending on your particular brand of faith, you could light a candle in the church or play the slot machines in Bundoran!

The place at that time was a fertile breeding ground for characters. Tommy 'Gregory' Mc Govern, who had a shop opposite Mac's field, was a real breath of fresh air with his contagious good humour and 'gift of the gab'. Like Pat Doonan, another local wit, he was full of devilment and always 'on the cod'. He loved 'taking a hand' at people and could keep an army 'in swithers'. He 'brought the house down' whenever he took to the stage.

John Kirwan, the shoemaker, was also one with special appeal. As he said himself, his was a 'Wait a While' rather than a 'While you Wait' shop and this was reflected in the array of shoes, old brogues, wellingtons, harnesses, clocks and watches, umbrellas and wirelesses that lay around, patiently awaiting his attention. He could turn his hand to anything - tie flies, cut

Pee Cassidy's 'Bar and Grocery', Main Street. Inset, Pee Cassidy corking stout.

hair, fix a leaking saucepan, stitch anything that was stitchable and stick anything that was stickable. He was a gifted storyteller – in the mould of Munchausen – and a wonderful fisherman. Not surprising, his tall yarns flowed freely as he pulled hard on a wax end or hammered away on his last! Of course, John didn't pick up his talents off the ground. His father, Andy, before him – also a gifted shoemaker- could leave you marvelling as he recalled his amazing exploits. When 'at himself' he had no trouble making the round trip to Enniskillen by cart-wheel in record time – could leave home after mid-day, conduct all his business and still have at least two pairs of shoes soled and heeled before the Angelus bell rang out at six! John's good wife, Maggie, must have had the patience of Job to put up with the steady stream of visitors that paraded right through her kitchen en route to John's workshop at the back. How she managed to get through her work and deal with the influx at the same time, we'll never know. She had a kind word for everyone and there was always tea in her pot and a welcoming stool by her fireside.

'Joe of the Forge' operated close to the river and Fair Green. Like John's, his was a welcoming place and a popular retreat or meeting-point, especially for farmers 'of a wet day'. We loved to stand nearby and watch the flying sparks from the impact of his hammer on the red hot iron, or marvel at the way he could hold the horse's hoof between his knees, extract the nails with his pincers and rip off the old shoe. I also loved to see him thrust the newly shaped shoe into a barrel of water and listen to it hissing and spitting until cool.

Pat Woods, Postmaster

Sonny Mac mending a bike outside his shop alongside the New
Bridge while Mamie Reilly maintains a watching brief! (1949)
Photo: Mary Gallagher (nee McGovern)

Phil Mc Kiernan's bicycle shop with its smell of grease, cleaning solvent and musty rubber and array of black Raleigh bikes, as well as Jack the Butcher's ice-cold outlet with its sawdusty floor, were other social meeting places that contributed in their own way to the well-being of the community.

Of course, Woods's post-office, like the creamery, was quite central to life in the village. Here letters were sorted and local telephone subscribers were connected to the outside world by means of a switchboard. Not only did the office provide the full range of postal services, it also catered for the 'gear and tackle' needs of local fishermen. The Woods family, like many post-office proprietors at the time, went well beyond the call of duty in offering help and advice to their various customers. Elsewhere in the same building, a bank operated a sub-office. Here too, every Saturday morning, Miss Ellie Fitzpatrick from Milltown (a member of Tim Fitz's famous ceilidhe band) conducted piano and fiddle lessons in a room with a wall-hanging bearing the inscription, 'Today is the 'tomorrow' you worried about yesterday and all is well'. But for this good lady's infinite patience and kind understanding, I would have been tempted to question the veracity of the quotation, especially whenever my fiddle screeched and emitted some rather wayward sounds!

We had a book in Pee Cassidy's Bar and Grocery. This meant that we didn't have to pay on the nail for each item. We could get things on tick. That was just as well because as youngsters we seemed to spend a right while trotting up and down for messages – for a box of matches, a loaf of bread, flour, a pound of butter, lamp-oil, a quarter pound of tea and two pounds of sugar. Like most others, we had no fridge and there were no convenience foods. You bought as you needed it and cooked on the spot. Occasionally, you might have to get something out of the ordinary – 'clarendo' (now known as flaked maize) for the cows after calving or a dozen of stout for the men at the hay. The Cassidy girls, May and Ena, took a note of all purchases

Local GAA Historian, Andy Kelly

P.J. (Sonny) McHugh. Creamery manager

in the book, and our mother paid the bill in whole or in part periodically. As children we sensed that 'paying off Cassidys' was a big deal and a cause for celebration!

On the other hand, if the bill remained outstanding for some time – as happened whenever there was a bus strike, when two of our stock died of 'Black Leg' in the early 50's and had to be replaced, or when my father's wages were cut back due to shorter hours resulting from the main Enniskillen road being blown up in 1961 – my parents would get quite anxious. Making ends meet was an endless task for my mother and any unforeseeable setback was tantamount to disaster. You see at that time paying your way was regarded as something of a cardinal virtue. Keeping your good name was very important. You had to make sure that the question, 'What will the neighbours say?' didn't arise! Shops like Cassidy's for their part really appreciated your custom and expressed their thanks with a generous 'Christmas Box' each year. This might include a bottle of Sandeman's port, a fruit cake and some cigarettes.

In the 40's and 50's shops were more environmentally friendly than shops to day despite all the emphasis on white coats, sink units and so on. All the bottles were made of glass rather than plastic and grocery items such as tea, sugar, prunes, raisins and biscuits were packed there and then into reusable or disposable paper bags. Most people of that generation will have a very vivid memory of the strong black sugar bags. Meal came in large jute sacks that were used again and again. The tea arrived in large wooden chests lined with silver paper. Each contained 120 lbs., which was sorted and sold in pound, half- pound and quarter- pound units.

At that time the word 'recyclable' wasn't mentioned but it was the order of the day. The hand-me-down system then in vogue took care of any shoes, clothes etc. that still had a bit of life left in them. Anything that could be mended was. Socks were darned, trousers and jackets

The Church Road in winter.

were patched. You wouldn't dream of throwing away an egg carton and as for newspapers, they had a hundred and one uses from 'foddering' bums to keeping out draughts! Housewives made sheets and pillow-cases from the calico bags in which the flour came. Many a parent was delighted to get hold of an old tea-chest in which to pen a young child for a while. During the war, even the tea itself was sometimes re-cycled.

Whenever you'd go up the street someone or other would refer to the weather. People had a real obsession with it. I suppose that was hardly surprising since it impinged to such an extent on the basic issues of saving the turf, winning the hay and drying clothes. Silence prevailed while the forecast was being read out on the wireless even though comments were often made that those in Dublin knew 'damn all', were only 'chancing their arm' and were more often wrong than right. Old Moore's view, the direction of the wind, apparent distance of the mountains (if Ben Aughlin looked near, you could expect rain), cloud formation, the colour of the sky at night or in the morning, the movement and sounds of birds and animals, the quality and quantity of red berries on the holly and many other signs and possible omens were analysed for enlightenment. A white ring around the moon was a sign of storm. Once corns began to 'act up' everyone knew that the rain was on its way. If it fell on St. Swithin's day, you knew you shouldn't venture out without your umbrella for forty days.

Despite all their signs and omens, few predicted the big snow-fall in 1947. The really harsh weather that year began in February. A fierce blizzard set in on the Monaghan Day fair of Mohill (Feb. 25) and continued non-stop for twenty four hours, creating huge drifts from nine to fifteen feet high in places. There was no sign of a thaw for weeks. Swanlinbar was completely isolated, with no newspapers, telephones, or post, no buses running and provisions in the shops at an all-time low. More than a thousand sheep were reported missing in the area. As late as June, there was still snow lying behind some hedges.

People often cursed the weather by saying, 'Bad cess to it!' but it did in fact create a common bond. Everyone claimed to be something of a weather expert. One might remark with a serious air of authority that there would be 'damn all rain' while another might add that he didn't really like the look of the sky, but to dismiss another person's viewpoint out of hand would have been considered a serious affront to his intelligence and could draw upon you his eternal wrath.

Looking back, you cannot but marvel at the fullness and variety of life in that one small village. 'Twould prompt you to re-echo Mary Hopkin's words in the late '60's, 'Those were the Days'.

Jack 'The Butcher'

SATURDAY, 13th JANUARY 1951 ———————

1.0 p.m.: Records. 1.15: Donnelly's Programme. 1.30: News. 1.40: Bird's Programme. 1.55-2.30: Gramophone Concert. 5.30: Billy the Woodturner's Cat." 5.40: Novelty Numbers on Two Pianos. 5.55: Interlude. 6.0: The Angelus. 6.01: Making and Mending. 6.20: Interlude. 6.30: News and Announcements. 6.50: Interlude. 6.55: Here's The Doctor. 7.0: Sea Shanties. 7.15: Rome-Paris-New York. 7.45: Ridire na Gealai. 8.15: Records. 8.45: Ivy Day: A feature about Parnell and Parnellites. 9.20: Meet the Pheasant. 9.40: Farmers' Feature. 9.55: Nuacht. 10.10: News. 10.30: Hospitals' Trust Programme. 11.0: Close Down.

SUNDAY, 14th JANUARY

10.30-11.15 a.m.: High Mass from Gort Mhuire, Dundrum. 1.0 p.m.: Orchestras of the World: Denmark. 2.0-2.30: Lunchtime Concert. 5.30: Broadcast Music of the Week. 5.55: Interlude. 6.0: The Angelus. 6.01: Programme by Mobile Recording Unit. 6.30: News. 6.45: Appeal on behalf of St. Brigid's Orphanage, Dublin. 6.50: Soccer Survey by Ronnie Walsh. 7.0: More Covent Garden Memories. 7.30: "Beginners Please." 8.05: Irish Dance Music: Leo Rowsome's Pipes Quartet. 8.30: "Robinson Crusoe": Pantomime. 9.30: Provincial News Round-up. 9.50: Readings from the Old Testament. 10.0: News. 10.15: Gaelic Sports News. 10.30: Hospitals' Trust Programme. 11.0: Close Down.

MONDAY, 15th JANUARY

1.0 p.m.: Records. 1.15: Mitchelstown Creameries' Programme

1.30: News. 1.40: "Radio Review" Programme. 1.55-2.30: Lunchtime Concert. 5.30: Children at the Microphone. 5.40: Gunnairi an Rio Grande. 5.55: Interlude. 6.0: The Angelus. 6.01: Feilire na Naomh. 6.10: Deireadh na Seilge. 6.30: News. 6.50: Interlude. 6.55: Maura O'Connor (Mezzo-Soprano). 7.10: Between the Bookends. 7.30: Popular Concert: Radio Eireann Light Orchestra. 8.30: Poetry. 8.50: Cor De Groot (Piano). 9.25: "My Kind of Music" in which listeners present some of their favourite records. 9.55: Nuacht. 10.10: News. 10.30: Hospitals' Trust Programme. 11.0: Close Down.

TUESDAY, 16th JANUARY

1.0 p.m.: Records. 1.15: Donnelly's Programme. 1.30: News. 1.40: Bird's Programme. 1.55-2.30: Gramophone Concert. 5.30: An Oige Go Deo. 5.45: Amhrain: Olive Kelly. 5.55: Interlude. 6.0: The Angelus. 6.01: An Stroinseir —Sceal. 6.10: Records. 6.30: News. 6.50: Interlude. 6.55: Leo Rowsome (Uilleann Pipes). 7.10: Tuairimi Is Tuairisci. 7.25: Records. 7.45: An Irish Folklorist in Indiana: A Talk. 8.0: Orchestral Concert. 9.0: Tuesday Review. 9.40: Talking of Ireland, 2: Inisfail and her Golden Ages: A Talk by Madame Maud Gonne Mac Bride. 9.55: Nuacht. 10.10: News. 10.30: Hospitals' Trust Programme. 11.0: Close Down.

WEDNESDAY, 17th JANUARY

1.0 p.m.: Hospitals' Requests. 1.30: News. 1.40-2.30: Hospitals' Requests. 5.30: Drawing and Painting. 5.45: Songs for Children. 5.55: Interlude. 6.0: The

Radio Eireann programmes 1951.

From Athlone to Montrose

I once heard a story about a Monaghan man who was a bit deaf. Whenever he felt low or a 'wee bit run down', his catch-cry was always, 'Turn up Artlone'! Indeed the wireless or transistor (when it arrived in the late '50's) was a real lifeline for half the country including the good citizens of Swanlinbar.

2RN began to broadcast on a regular basis on January 1 1926, but wasn't available throughout the land. A high powered station (initially 60Kw) was later established in Athlone in 1932 to coincide with the Eucharistic Congress. 2RN and its Cork 'side-kick' then became known as Radio Athlone. It in turn changed to Radio Eireann in 1938. The new radio centre at Montrose was completed in 1971 and live radio broadcasts from there began in September 1973.

In 1949 there were just seven hours of broadcasting a day, the afternoon slot – 1 to 2.30 and the evening slot – 5.30 to 11pm but in 1952 a morning niche was added. Apart from Micheál O' Hehir on a Sunday afternoon and Sean Óg O' Ceallaghán's Sports Results that night , people listened in to every news and weather bulletin, in fact to every kind of programme from Radio Eireann's opening tune, 'O'Donnell Abu', until late at night. It was the wireless that brought the great music of the world and all the big stories of the day into most kitchens. It told people that the war was over (1945), that Hilary and Tenzing had climbed Mount Everest (1953), that Roger Bannister ran a mile in less than four minutes (1954), that Ronnie Delaney captured the gold in Melbourne {1956}, that the Russians had launched their Sputnik (1957) and that Liam Whelan and seven of his team mates had lost their lives in the Munich air disaster (February 1958). People really enjoyed 'Hospitals's Requests' and 'Between Ourselves', which was presented by Radio Eireann's chief newsreader and Head Announcer, Kathleen Dolan, whom Louis Mac Neice described as 'The Golden Voice of Ireland'.

We had 'The Foley Family' and Din Joe in 'Take the Floor' (which came on air in 1953 and continued until 1965) inviting us to 'lift the latch, open the door, step right in and take the floor'. His programme featured seanachai, Eamon Kelly, the Garda band, Tommy Dando on the organ as well as Rory O' Connor and his troupe of step dancers. There was the old time favourite, Paddy Crosbie and his 'School around the Corner' and of course, 'Living With Lynch' (1954) featuring Joe Lynch (who later starred in 'Bracken' and 'Glenroe' as 'Dinny Byrne'), 'The Rambling House' with Eamon Kelly as host, singers Teresa Clifford and Sean O' Siochain and actor Eamon Keane.

Who could forget Walton's with Leo Maguire's reminder, 'if you feel like singing, do sing an Irish song' – 'the songs our fathers loved'. We heard about Donnolly's sausages being 'double wrapped for double protection' and all about Michelstown creamery, 'the home of good cheese'. There was 'The Maureen Potter Show' with the diminutive artist and 'Christee'. Sometimes as 'Ag-enn-es' she had us all in stitches shouting for 'Jeh-ehm'!

'Question Time' with Eric Boden or Joe Linnane came on air that night and was followed later by the 'Thomas Davis Lectures' produced by Francis Mc Manus. Sean O Morchu presented his 'Teach-a-Ceili' on Saturday night while 'The Kennedys of Castlerosse' (Radio Eireann's first soap opera that ran from April 1955 until 1975) brightened up the day from 1p.m. to 1.15p.m. Written by Hugh Leonard, David Hanly and Kevin Fuller, the cast included Marie Keane, Pat Laffan and Philip O' Flynn. You wouldn't get a word in edgeways while they were on air. Then there was that very popular children's series on painting, 'Art Adventures with Sean Bunny and Marion King'. Few programmes generated more excitement than the annual Aintree Grand National with the familiar voice of Micheal O'Hehir covering the section from Beecher's Brook to the Canal Turn.

While most sets remained on 'Athlone', some did switch occasionally to the B.B.C, and enjoyed such programmes as 'Housewives' Choice', 'Woman's Hour', 'The Archers', 'Take it from Here', 'The Goons' and of course, 'Mrs. Dale's Diary'. My mother invariably listened to the classified football results read by James Alexander Gordon on 'Sports Report' every Saturday evening at 5p.m. Silence descended on our kitchen as the Central Band of the RAF introduced the five minute slot with the sounds of 'Out of the Blue'. It wasn't that my mum was a soccer fanatic, but the Y.P. pools were based on these results and she was always hoping against hope that one day she would hit the jackpot. In this way, I became very familiar with clubs high and low from North to South, but I must admit that there was a time when I would have appreciated how one lad thought that 'Partick Thistle Nil' was the name of one of these.

Young people at that time were 'hooked' on Radio Luxemburg, 'The Station of the Stars, broadcasting live from the Grand Duchy on 208 metres Medium wave and 49 metres on the Shortwave'. 'Fab 208', as it was known, came on air away back in 1933. Stephen Williams was its first disc jockey. The Germans took it over for some time during the war,but when it resumed we all tuned in to join disc jockeys such as Pete Murray, Jimmy Saville, Noel Edmonds, David 'Kid' Jensen and Tony Prince ('Your Royal Ruler'). The 'Top Twenty' was launched in 1948 and with Teddy Johnston and Pete Murray at the helm it became (like Alan Freeman's 'Pick of The Pops' on B.B.C. Radio on Sunday afternoon) compulsive listening on a Sunday night. Jimmy Saville joined up in 1957 and during his nine years with 208 he won the coveted 'Top British D.J. award eight times. David Jacobs hosted 'The Honeymoon Show', which was sponsored by Fyffes. 'Take Your Pick' (1955-1968) with Michael Miles captured an audience of over seven million.

Most people from that era will remember one particular advertisement. It was Horace Batchelor claiming he could help listeners win the football pools with his 'Infra Draw' (or was it 'In For A Draw') method. All you had to do was write to him at Department 1, Keynsham (that's K-E-Y-N-S-H-A-M), Bristol. Poor old Horace died in 1981, ten years before Luxembourg closed down, leaving behind happy memories of innocent times when we enjoyed listening to his voice and the music of 208 fading and returning on our transistors as we snuggled beneath the dormitory blankets!

Servicing the wireless in the early days was a bit of a nuisance. You had to have two batteries - a two volt lead acid chargeable accumulator or wet battery, and a high tension or dry deck battery. The former, a tall glass affair with a metal handle, had to be topped up regularly in a garage. This normally cost around five to six pence. It was imperative to get this job done in advance of any major event such as an Ulster or All-Ireland final. Otherwise, tempers could get a little frayed.

Living close to the border gave us access to television even before our own national service came on air in '61. When the B.B.C. activated its Divis transmitter in July 1955, it could be seen north of a line from Sligo to Wicklow. When Ulster Television followed in October 1959 those of us living along the border had a good choice of programmes. Youngsters could enjoy 'Watch with mother', 'The Appleyards', 'Bill and Ben-The Flower-pot men' (1951), 'The Woodentops ' with their 'Peas for dinner! Peas for dinner', Muffin the Mule, Andy Pandy, Sooty and his Xylophone, Eamon Andrew's 'Crackerjack'(1955) (at five to five every Friday),'Lenny the Lion' (1956) 'Meet the Penguins', 'Jungle Boy', 'Pinky and Perky'(1957), 'Blue Peter' (1958) and 'The Bumbles'. Teenagers had 'Six Five Special' (1957) and of course 'Juke Box Jury' (1959) with David Jacobs and his friend Marleen (of 'Oil give it five' fame!). Cathy Mc Gowan, the young girl assistant with her long straight hair, was there to add a touch of glamour to the proceedings!

There was a host of other memorable programmes including 'What's My Line'(1951), 'The Good Old Days' and Panorama (1953), Jack Warner's 'Dixon of Dock Green', 'This is Your Life' and 'The Brains Trust'(1955), Hancock's Half Hour and 'The Lone Ranger' starring Clayton Moore (1956), 'Emergency Ward 10', 'The Benny Hill Show', 'On Safari' and 'The Sky at Night(1957), 'The London Palladium', 'White Heather Club' and 'The Black and White Minstrels' (!958). Then there was 'Double Your Money' with Hughie Green, 'Tonight' with Cliff Michelmore, 'Scotland Yard', and 'Lunchbox'. Peggy Mount and David Kossoff starred in 'The Larkins' from 1958 to 1964. There was also David Attenborough's 'Zoo Quest' and lots of humour and light relief from comedian, Benny Hill, and magicians, David Nixon and Tommy Cooper.

The television advertisements introduced in 1955, were then seen as novelty items. We learned about Murray Mints, 'the too-good-to- hurry mints', Double Diamond that 'works wonders', 'Turkish Delight, full of Eastern promise' and 'Cadum for Madam'. There was the big six mark question, 'Can you tell Stork from butter?' and Hughie Green came on rooting for 'White Tide'. 'Don't forget the Fruit Gums, Mum!'arrived in 1956 and 'The Esso sign means happy motoring' was hot on its heels in '57. We were reminded that 'you're never alone with a Strand' while Domestos even then was 'killing all known germs'.

Telefis Eireann came on air at 7p.m. on December 31st 1961 with an opening address by President de Valera and messages from Cardinal Conway and Sean Lemass. A concert from the Gresham Hotel, hosted by the television chairman, Eamon Andrews, followed. His guests that night included Patrick O' Hagan, the Artane Boys' Band and Micheál O'Hehir. We got our last glimpse of innocent Ireland!

Telifis opened up a whole new world, especially for those who didn't as yet have access to the English and Northern Ireland channels. Topics hitherto classified as 'taboo' were now openly discussed and old assumptions were questioned publicly on programmes such as Gay Byrne's 'Late, Late Show'. Hair cracks began to surface on our cocoons. Soon we would find ourselves exposed to the winds of change.

The 'Bargain King' (Cyril Chapman). He could entertain young and old with his 'gift of the gab'. Photo Joe Chapman, Bundoran.

CREATING A STIR

The village was generally quiet but for many people this wasn't a major problem. Older folk would probably have agreed with neighbouring writer, John Mc Gahern, when he noted in his 'Memoir' that 'the best of life is lived quietly, where nothing happens but our calm journey through the day, where change is imperceptible and the precious life is everything.'

However, the place did come to life on occasions e.g. when the 3.30p.m.bus would unload its cardboard cartons of chirpy 'Day Old Chicks' (13/6 a doz.) from Mc Cormack's Elm Bank hatchery in Cavan. The Guinness men broke the silence at other times as they plopped their large wooden barrels onto their straw-filled sacks before rolling them into the bottling stores. Then there was the rattling of bottles when 'Cavan Mineral Waters' arrived in town.

At night—especially on a Sunday night when northern pubs were closed- revellers from across the border would arrive in droves for a bit of 'divarshun' and the cheap 'Free State' beer. If undisturbed by the 'law', they would sit contentedly in the local taverns skulling pints until the early hours , knowing that the more they drank, the more they saved! The guards seldom bothered except when there was a particularly officious sergeant in charge, anxious to show that their remit extended beyond implementing the Dog Licence and the 1936 Noxious Weed Act, cutting tongues out of dead foxes and 'doling out' seventeen and sixpence rewards, reading rain gauges, tending to census forms, checking on parents who didn't send their children to school regularly, or 'pulling' cyclists for not having lights on their bicycles. However, it was the election, fair day or the arrival of a circus that really brought the place to life.

Politics was viewed as a very serious business in those days. There may not have been coloured photos of well-groomed candidates every few yards along your way, or cavalcades touring the constituency, but 'after Mass on Sunday' speeches in the Chapel Square were more than adequate to rouse the party faithful and call on board at least some of those wavering in the aisles. In most cases, however, whole families tended to vote along the same lines as their ancestors. Civil war politics were still very much in vogue. We had a General Election every few years back then – in 1943, 1944, 1948, 1951, 1954 and 1957.

Before the congregation would emerge from Second Mass, an outgoing T.D. or Senator would be ready to join some local committee men (- the women had to go home to make the Sunday dinner!) on the back of Mick's lorry while others, who 'lived for the party', would be on standby to mingle with the crowd and act as cheerleaders. Soon proceedings would be in full swing. 'Don't change horses when crossing the stream' or 'we did it before and we'll do it again', would be bellowed out from on high. The odd heckler might retort, 'What about the yella butter' or 'Get them out, get them out' Others would chant 'Hear, hear' or was it 'Here, here'! I was never really sure!

The Sinn Fein speeches before the election in March 1957 (after Sean Mac Bride of Clann na Poblachta 'pulled the plug' on the John A. Costello-led Coalition government) were the best of all. We were exhorted to vote Pat Duffy No. 1 and vote for the others according to our choice. 'Occupied Ulster', 'Our six counties' 'the British presence', 'the B-Specials', 'British Crown forces', 'Pearse and Tone' and 'this land the State calls Free' all got an airing. Before their meetings ended, you'd be ready to go down the Enniskillen road and do your bit for Ireland! 70,000 others were also impressed for they elected four new Sinn Fein T.D.'s including the highly popular John Joe Mc Girl from neighbouring Ballinamore, Eanachan O' hAnluain (Fergal's brother), Monaghan, Ruairi Ó Brádaigh, Longford/Westmeath and John Joe Rice, South Kerry. Feelings were running high after the deaths of Sean South and Fergal O' Hanlon during the attack on Brookeborough barracks the previous January. 40,000 turned up for South's funeral in Limerick and something approaching a state of national mourning prevailed for some time.

Of course, we had our own mock election campaigns. In retrospect, our rallying call – 'we come before you to stand behind you to tell you something we know nothing about' was possibly a more honest appraisal of the situation than what we heard from some of our adult leaders!

We read in Samuel Lewis's 'Topographical Dictionary of Ireland' that fairs were held in Swad on Feb.2, March 30, May 18, June 29, July 27, Aug.18, Sept. 3 and 29, October 26 and Dec.1 and 29, but in my day most took place on the 14th.of each month. Farmers with their Shorthorns and white-headed Herefords and sack-covered horse-carts of grunting Large White pigs and squealing bonhams, as well as jobbers in heavy high-laced red boots with ash plants, bamboo canes or knobbed blackthorns, would start streaming into the village between 8a.m. and 9a.m. Cant men would set up their stalls of second-hand clothes, tools, harness, ropes etc. on the footpaths. There would be fresh 'herns' (herrings) for sale, all 'alive with their eyes open, pipes in their mouths and them all smoking' – a nice change from the fellows preserved in the barrels of brine - and also Early York or Flat Dutch cabbage plants in the springtime. You might even see the odd tinker getting organized with his line-up of porringers or small milk cans. If the 'Bargain King' (Cyril Chapman) turned up, he'd entertain old and young with his 'gift of the gab'. He would hold up one item, add another and finally a third. Then he would announce that he wasn't going to charge £1 or 10 shillings or even 5 shillings. He would throw in yet another item and invite someone from his captive audience to take the whole 'damn lot' out of his sight for half a crown. He would claim to have the cure for receding hair, corns, warts, and awkward husbands or wives, as well as scissors, pen knives of brightest Ruhr steel, hair-clippers, the very best of saws, screwdrivers and wrenches, all made in Germany by the Boys of Wexford and flown in that very morning at enormous expense. He even had a consignment of Mac's Smile blades specially designed 'to snip the mother-in-law's throat'!

It was interesting to watch the bargaining and haggling. In those days there were no blue cards, no Department officials and no worries about horns that should have been removed. The cattlemen would go about prodding and feeling the animals' 'haunches' (or hip bones), scattering them 'to get a good look', offering ridiculous prices or making derogatory remarks about some 'scraggy calf that never got his fill'! Then they would walk away giving the impression that the farmer was 'off his rocker' and hadn't a clue. Farmers, who heard it all

Street up!

before, wouldn't take any heed of this. They didn't want to be told later on that they had been 'codded up to their two eyes' or that they 'saw ye comin'. Later, the jobber might return and his 'tangler' (an 'impartial' intermediary between buyer and seller) would suggest that they 'split the difference' and 'make the dale'. If this proved to be acceptable, the buyer would spit on his hand and with a shout slap it down on the owner's palm. Money would be paid and a 'luck penny' (anything from one to five shillings) given. The poor 'bastes', now under different ownership and somewhat mesmerized by it all, would then be moved blindly along, their waterfalls of 'skitter' spewing forth and splattering their new and uncertain paths. Once more the air would resound to a fresh crescendo of shouting, haggling, swearing and wielding of sticks.

Afterwards when the bargains were all made, farmers would retire to Lily Keenan's or Ellen Reilly's 'Eatin' houses for a feed of roast beef, spuds, peas, cabbage or mashed turnip and a jug of brown gravy with a 'lock' of onions, or just tea and a sandwich or a couple of buns and a cut of ginger cake. Most would head to the public houses for a few bottles of stout or a 'half-one', and those who didn't touch the 'stuff' except on special occasions would often get caught up in arguments or be 'rarin' for a fight. Occasionally, an emancipated woman might drop into some snug (a tiny room with intimate seating for the more sedate drinkers who wished to imbibe unseen) for a small sherry or port, but generally speaking the women left the men to themselves so that they could get on with meeting friends and acquaintances they hadn't seen for an age.

Late in the evening you would see the odd character with the peak of his cap to the back, herrings wrapped in newspaper under his oxter, and he shouting or calling on Paddy Reilly in a hiccuppy way to return to Ballyjamesduff. No doubt the same fellow would have been blissfully unaware of the fact that Paddy, Percy French's famous jarvey, had died at the age of 88 in October '39. He would go slipping or staggering through the streets, now littered with baked and half-baked cakes of dung – sometimes with a highly-embarrassed wife or 'gossoon' in tow. Another, without a worry in the world and sprawled out 'blotto' across the back of a cart, might let his donkey take the initiative and chauffeur him home. With reins lying slack, his limp body would rock and roll to the movements of the cart.

The biggest fairs of all were the hiring fairs. These were usually held twice a year in May and November but the main fair in Swad in the 1950's at least took place on June 29, the feast day of St. Peter and Paul. Hiring, which dated back to the time of the Ulster Plantation, had more or less died out completely by the late '40's to early '50's due to major social and economic changes in Irish farming in the 1930's and 1940's. The Economic War in the 30's, the introduction of the Ford Ferguson tractor in 1941 and the arrival of the Ferguson Standard, David Brown and later on, the Massey Ferguson, cut down drastically on the need for farm labourers. My father could recall well-to-do northern farmers 'weighing up' the walk and appearance of young prospective workers, questioning them about their age, work experience and examining their hands and muscles as their apprehensive parents looked on. They in turn sought assurance that their son or daughter would get a decent wage, have a comfortable bed and be treated well.

The six month hiring fee varied somewhat. In the 1930's and early 1940's, girls got about £8, general farm labourers £10 while ploughmen could demand the princely sum of £16! Children from large families were often sent out of dire necessity to be hired in order to pay for rent and food. Is it any wonder the hiring fairs were sometimes called 'slave markets'? 'Earnest money' (usually one shilling) was given to the prospective employee to indicate that the deal was sealed. Those hired normally didn't get paid until the end of their six month term. If they left early, they didn't get any remuneration at all. If their service was deemed to be satisfactory, they were given the option of remaining on for a further six months. Few tears were shed when the practise of hiring died out. Ordinary fairs would soon follow suit and be replaced by livestock marts. Their demise brought to an end what had been part and parcel of life for countless Irish generations.

While the fairs brought a bit of life to the locality, there was nothing quite like a good circus to lift one's spirit on to a higher plane. The whole place would be abuzz when Fossett's, Sandow's or Duffy's, with their heavy trailers and colourful vans and caravans, would roll in the Bawn road, set up their big top with its fluttering flags in Mac's lawn and, as the posters promised, present 'The Greatest Show on Earth'!

An advert in 'The Fermanagh Herald' in 1956 described John Duffy's circus in less exaggerated terms initially as 'The Greatest Show on Irish soil' but then added that it had 'the cream of the circus world', that it was 'the greatest show of them all with everything new but the name!'

Fossetts had a certain affiliation with Swad. Just before World War 2 they decided, as a marketing strategy, to rename their outfit 'Heckenberg's Berlin Tower Super Circus'. When the war did break out, they happened to be in Derry. Some locals didn't take too kindly to their 'German' visitors and stoned them out of the city! They didn't stop until they crossed the border at Swad and enlisted some locals to help them repair their vans. Needless to say, they reverted to their original name overnight.

Those troubled days were far from our minds as we dangled our legs from high seats inside their sawdusty tent and red-nosed clowns entertained us royally as they tried to balance on single wheels while performing dogs pushed their dolls' prams around the ring. There were high-stepping horses and high wire acts by weather beaten-men and gorgeous looking, scantily clad, glittering girls who sent those of us in the senior classes headlong on our first passionate flights. They moved in tune with the brass band but not with those times! Next morning they were all on the road again while we were back at our ink-wells trying to 'get a handle' on 'covet and 'calumny' ('contraception' still hadn't been discovered!) or some aspects of the sixth and ninth commandments!

Lucy Connaughton (inset) with her husband Joe and their Uragh scholars, 1950 (Photo: Ben Mc Hugh)

TO SCHOOL BY THE CREAMERY

Beyond the creamery brae that led to town,
Where oft a cart in panic trundled down,
There with his 'wand' to help him 'keep the cool',
Joe, 'The Master', ran his two-roomed school.

'Tempus fugit'. It seems but yesterday since I threw my school bag across my back, left my home beneath Ben Aughlin and the Cuilcagh mountains, to join Cassidys, Cullens, Dolans, Gilleeces, Gormans, Keenans, Kirwans, Leonards, Leydons, Mc Governs, McHughs, Maguires, Morrises, O'Briens, Priors, Scollans et al for yet another day in the Master's 'noisy mansion'. This was situated close to the local creamery, about half way between the village and the parish cemetery at Killaghaduff. It too was a place of constant churning and separating where you could sometimes feel you were half way between this life and the next!

Most of us made the journey by 'Shank's mare'. In those days you might have been 'driven' to school, but it would have been unthinkable for anyone to get 'dropped at the gate' by car. During the warm summer days of June and early July, we loved to discard our shoes or heavy hobnailed boots and go barefooted, bursting the tar bubbles as we went through the village street. We also enjoyed the feel of squelchy mud, but the odd stubbing of a toe or prick of a thorn was not much 'craic'.

Occasionally, Tommie Breen, who collected our milk and took it to the creamery on his donkey and cart, would invite me on board. I would then lace the straps of my school bag around one of the small protruding shafts at the back and hop on. As Tommie issued his 'Click-click-click', 'Giddy-up' or 'Gee-up-there' and the cart with its narrow, wavering, iron rimmed wheels cracked along, I'd watch the ground fly past and listen to the jingle of tackle and the sound of bouncing cans. I'd either sit with my legs dangling from the back or else take my place on one of the smaller cans.

It wasn't exactly luxury travel but in time, old car wheels with high mileage tyres would bring ass transport into the twentieth century and facilitate a more bum- friendly creamery cruise. At times, depending on his mood, Tommie might give me a chance to handle the reins. With legs astride, I'd put on a bit of a show, leading with one hand and waving to my envious, dilly-dallying school mates with the other. I might try to speed things up a little, but Breen's ass was a creature of habit and not given to heroics. He tended to spurn any amateurish attempt to change the status quo. Out of sheer malice, he would sometimes stall by way of giving me his own version of the two finger salute and would then suddenly and unexpectedly take off again in a flurry, intent on throwing me headlong over his crossed back.

On our way to school, we passed the usual daily mass-goers emerging from the Chapel Square and the morning paper addicts having a quick squint at the main headings, or death notices in the 'Independent' or 'Press', depending on their political persuasion. A notice on a wall at the turn for the school road had a rather succinct message:

Post no bills, play no balls,
Court no women on Kirwan's walls'.

At this time of day, there was usually a stream of carts, floats, tractors and vans moving along steadily towards the creamery. Established away back in 1905, it was a hive of industry and central to the well-being of the local economy. The farmers would climb the steps leading to a platform where they would empty their numbered cans and have their milk tested for bacteria and butterfat content.

Here Mr. Patrick J. ('Sonny') Mc Hugh held sway for over fifty years. He was assisted at different times by his son, Ben (who later took his place as creamery manager), by Paddy Mc Hugh (Mill Street), Fonsie Heavey (Commas) and Benny Maguire (Uragh). Sonny, like the ancient Roman emperors, wielded great power - he could give you the 'thumbs down' if everything wasn't in order. The price you received per gallon was determined by 'the test'. Once clear, you got your allocation of skim, which was used for baking bread and feeding calves and pigs.

If you peeped into the creamery itself you wouldn't hear your ears with the sound of shouting, hissing steam, belts and pulleys and the rolling of cans. You'd see men stoking the boiler with coal, lubricating the machinery and generally busying themselves. We loved to watch the thick cream streaming from the separator.

Farmers inclined to leave things to the last minute would be 'bustin their asses' to get to their creamery destination before Big Mick's lorry transported the cream to Killeshandra.

In the summer time, whenever the weather was fine, there would be a real sense of urgency in the air as farmers on edge hurried home to get to work in the bog or hayfield. On Sunday afternoon, people gathered behind the creamery for a different purpose – to while away the time playing 'Pitch and Toss'.

Uragh Boys, like most schools at that time, had just two teachers. 'The Master' and his wife, 'The Mistress', who was the infant teacher in the 'Wee Room', would arrive punctual as usual in their old black Ford Prefect and park along the laurel hedge. He would then proceed smartly with his well-worn, brown leather case to the front door where he would greet us formally in Irish and turn the great key. Before long, window shutters would be removed, the white delph ink-wells inset in the desks would be filled, twigs would be crackling and great billows of turf smoke would be puffing up the chimney from the huge open grate behind the Master's desk. That's how our parents respectfully referred to him and we did likewise within earshot but at a safe distance, more varied and derogatory terms were applied!

The primary purpose of the school fire was to roast the Master's backside. Its secondary function was to ensure that the rest of us didn't freeze to death! The sniffing at times seemed to indicate that such an end was imminent, but a succession of swipes across a woollen sleeve stemmed the flow and warded off the crisis!

We started off in 'Low Infants', proceeded to 'High Infants' and spent two further years in the same room before going into the Master. My recollection of the infant programme is somewhat blurred – a maze of A,B,C, etc., 'This is Kate the cat speaking', 'Run Tom, run Mary', a dog called 'Spot', following the tonic solfa , making letters and figures on our 'clairins' and rubbing them out with the 'glantóir', playing with 'marla' (plasticine) and farm animals (stored in a Jacob's Marietta biscuit tin) and reciting poems about twenty froggies going to school down beside a rushy pool.

There was another one called 'The Fairy Folk' by the Ballyshannon poet, William Allingham. It started off like this –

'Up the airy mountain,
Down the rushy glen,
We daren't go a-hunting
For fear of little men.'

We all drew the self-same one-dimensional houses, each with four windows duly crossed and a door in the middle. The smoke from the single chimney always went right while the path led straight to the front door. The poor Mistress had to compliment each of us in turn for his Leonardian creation!

Learning by rote was the order of the day. We used to rhyme off 'one and one are two, two and two are four (or a haon is a haon is a do, a do is a do is a ceathar) etc. Later on 'Transcription' became the biggest word in our vocabulary (that was long before 'Transubstantiation' put it in the shade!). We went on to Brown and Nolan 'Headline Copies' in which we had to imitate a style of writing already laid out there before us. It was 'God help anyone' unfortunate enough to let a big blob of ink drop on his page! We had to memorise various tables (Six ones are six, six twos are twelve etc.) and do 'Take Away/How Many Are Left' sums. Your ear could get a bit of a twist if you 'left' too many apples!

The Mistress was also the church organist and had a great love of music, as had her successor, Miss Martina Leamy from Cashel in Tipperary. They passed this love on to us, teaching us many songs such as 'Labhair an Teanga Gaeilge', Treasna na Dtonnta', 'Oró Mo Bháidín', 'Báidín Fheidhlimidh, 'Óro, Sé Do Bheatha 'Bhaile', 'Dóchas Linn Naomh Pádraig' and 'Beidh Aonach Amárach I gCondae an Chláir'. For some peculiar reason 'Bheir Mí Ó' stands out above all the others.

'Bheir mí óró, bhean ó,
Bheir mí óró, ó bhean í,
Bheir mí óró ó hó
Tá mé brónach 's tú í m' dhíth.

We also learned a whole variety of hymns - 'Bring Flowers of the Rarest', 'Hail Queen of Heaven, the Ocean Star' and 'Full in the Panting Heart of Rome'. The Mistress would start us off by hitting her tuning fork on the table and asking us to 'take that doh'. Sometimes she would accompany us on the harmonium.

On the odd occasion, she would tell us to 'get on with the work' and then take a look at herself in the mirror inside her 'cofra'. She would make a few adjustments here and there, powder her wrinkled face, tie her hair up in a bun and replace her hair netting. Then with a 'Where were we?' it was back to serious business again!

Most of the time she was very patient, sweet and motherly – fitted the title J.A.M - but occasionally when 'riz', she would 'fly off the handle', become a real demon and tell us we were nothing but a 'crowd of oul' 'glaiks'! We thought it was a phrase she herself created and while we didn't know exactly what she meant, we reckoned from her tone that it was anything but complimentary. Years later, thanks to Diarmaid Ó Muirithe's 'Words We Use', I discovered that a 'glaik' was a very old word that referred to one who deceives, one who stares in a rude manner or is particularly talkative. In retrospect, I'd say our Lucy wasn't too far off the mark, in fact she hit three in one.

The Master, an officer in the L.D.F. during 'The Emergency', was a staunch advocate of law and order and ruled his patch with an iron hand. He called out his military style instructions, 'Seasaigí', 'Iompaigí',' Gluaisigí' and it was just too bad if you failed to follow his commands! He had great faith in his well-seasoned hazel rod that was artistically pared at both ends, and when off duty lay resting on his table. This he christened his 'wand' and when in jocular mood, he would cite its medicinal attributes. If for any reason his 'wand' was out of commission, he would have to call on a crook-handled bamboo cane. This 'sub' generally didn't last long, became frayed at the end and had to be reduced and pensioned off as a 'pointer'. He reckoned that 'six of the best' from either weapon before, after, or even without a meal could work wonders.

If you ever forgot where you were and in a moment of weakness got involved in some 'skullduggery'(general devilment), such as flicking one of the pens with the 'two a penny' steel nibs into the wooden floor, pinning a compass point in the toe of your shoe and attempting to nudge it or a peann luaidhe up some protruding but unsuspecting 'tail-end', bending your ruler to launch an ink-laden 'cannonball' , playing 'noughts and crosses', inscribing your initials in the desk to guarantee immortality, or simply fidgeting with the ink-well cover, you were sure to see him peering over his dark, horn-rimmed glasses and beckoning you, with a twitch of his finger, to come forward for a closer encounter or more intimate exchange! If you did not see him immediately, you would soon gather, from the eerie silence all around, that someone was 'in for it'. Then to your horror, you would realise that that someone was you.

Sentence ('six of the best') and execution would follow in quick succession – like Pierpoint, he believed in instant dispatch! He would first of all touch your hand with the 'wand' to steady it or bring it to the required level and thus ensure that he didn't miss the 'runway' upon descent! With eyes firmly focused on your unfortunate paw, he would raise the instrument and his right leg simultaneously before coming down with all his might. The swish of the wand and its burning pain seemed to overlap. If he got you on the thumb it was particularly sore. You would be forced to wriggle your hand about for coolant purposes or nurse it tightly under your armpit before holding out again for the next instalment. It was imperative not to cry. That would give the Master infinite satisfaction and lower your standing amongst your peers. The lines appearing on your palm after the session used indicate whether you had been promoted to the rank of corporal or sergeant! There was a widely held belief that if you put horse-hair on the palm of your hand, the cane or 'wand' would split in two but no one in my time at least was prepared to test its veracity. On one occasion a particular scholar refused to take his 'medicine' and instead took flight across the desk tops with Master Joe in hot pursuit. We were highly entertained as he specified how his father would deal with the Master. I don't know anything about the evening sequel, but Connaughton was 6-0 ahead by the time the bell rang at 3 p.m.!

At that time few would enlighten their parents with regard to the number of 'slaps' they received in school, since they knew full well that little sympathy but rather the opposite would be forthcoming. Modern readers might jump to the conclusion that the Master was a violent man with a cruel streak. This wasn't the case. His actions must be viewed in their historical context. He was of his time, trained and practised in the old mode in those pre kid-glove, pre-Spock, pre child-centred 'Lugs' Brannigan days, when children were supposed to be seen and not heard, when people genuinely believed that suffering and discipline were prerequisites to progress. There was no talk then of embracing and celebrating your child's uniqueness! Teachers weren't instructed to 'endorse children's self-esteem'! Physical punishment (a 'clip on the ear', 'a belt across the lug', a good 'skelping' 'a toe up behind' etc.) was regarded as the normal antidote to unsocial or unacceptable behaviour. We know from the novels and works of writers such as John Mc Gahern and Frank Mc Court that there was widespread tolerance of brutality in the home and elsewhere at that time. The Master didn't have the benefit of modern psychological 'enlightenment', just an inherent belief, simplistic perhaps, that if he was meticulous with regard to 'correcting' our work and planning his lessons and 'kept our heads to the grind', we would progress, get life a little easier than our parents and forefathers and not have to 'dig ditches', 'lean on the shovel' or 'take the boat to England'. Sadly, there were other factors at play then that thwarted his dream.

Poverty and unemployment were rampant in those post-war years. A large percentage of his past pupils, trapped by this poverty and inequality, had no option but to leave Ireland and seek their fortunes elsewhere. The curriculum at the time didn't cater all that well for their needs. While the Master and many of his contemporary colleagues dispensed punishment fairly and squarely and didn't differentiate between scholars from different backgrounds, they didn't cater all that well for those with limited academic ability who found life in school quite intolerable and whose parents often needed them to help out with the farmwork at home. Thankfully, many of these, blessed with other great talents, shed the badge of 'dunce' and got on exceptionally well. Some, however, deprived of self-esteem, found it next to impossible to reach a higher rung.

Our school was known as Uragh Boys and Girls N.S. when it first opened in 1846, just one year after the Great Famine began. The girls got their own premises some fifty years later. Here, Miss Lily Mc Caffrey, a formidable figure, kept 'smacht' on the senior girls. Mrs Cassie Brennan, a lady 'to her finger-tips', looked after the 'wee' ones.

Uragh Boys was a two roomed white-washed shack with porches that served as cloakrooms attached at either end. Here in inclement weather we used to eat our lunches – thick slices of bread with sugar sprinkled on top, or jam and butter Farmer's loaf sandwiches, wrapped in bread paper, to be washed down with milk or cold tea from a newspaper 'corked' Chef or Guinness bottle. Afterwards, by way of diversion, you could find yourself being tossed over and back in the confined area, or trampled on trampled coats. For at least half the year, this place reeked of that lethal tripartite concoction generated by damp coats, stale bread and human flatulence!

Large wall-maps graced the walls of the Master's room. These were suspended from giant wooden spools, integral parts of a primitive but effective pulley system that allowed the maps to be raised or lowered at will. There were other home-made charts illustrating Irish grammatical endings and colourful nature presentations by Shell. There was also a well-worn black notice board ('Clar on lae'} on which the Master wrote the day's date and number in attendance. An old clock with Roman numerals-supposedly as old as the school itself- ticked out the time. Whenever it slowed down, the Master doused its pendulum section with paraffin to revive its drooping spirit, but it would have taken more than paraffin to make it move as fast as we wished! The cracked windows facing north looked out on the junior playground and further on, the River Blackwater.

Occasionally, when those of us 'in the same book' were standing in a row along the wall, we would be 'tickled pink' if we spied some farmer 'jouk down' to perform the very normal act of relieving himself behind the apparent coverage of the Blackwater (or Long) bridge opposite the creamery, completely oblivious to our gaze! We got a somewhat similar 'kick' when some unfortunate scholar with an excessive amount of gas in his alimentary canal passed wind at a particularly inappropriate moment! Weren't we a right shower to be so easily amused? Don't forget that these little incidents, and the occasional visits of the local priest, Diocesan Examiner, a travelling magician, cigire (inspector) or local School Attendance Garda, were our only real diversions from the ordinary daily routine.

Out the back, there was an old tumbledown shed for sticks, coal and turf. Close by was the dry 'Dull go G' leithreas (or lav), neither flush nor plush, I might add. Cornered with cob-webs, creepy crawlies and the like, it had a cut-out aperture in its wide, home-made seat through which you discarded your load before the pungent odour and fanfare of cleggs and their relations prompted a hasty withdrawal, and left you fit for nothing but a quick 'drag' on an oul' Woodbine! Along the walls of the school there were flowerbeds of lupines and neglected rosebushes, well-soaked with water from the broken gutters.

When the weather was fine, we generally played soccer or Gaelic. That's not to say that we didn't ever venture out onto a mucky pitch in inclement weather. Whenever we did that, we usually returned to class breathless, reeking of sweat and covered in 'clauber'. 'Prison' was also popular. Some scoured the play-ground for prospective detainees while 'screws' remained on guard in front of the laurel jail. Playing conkers, marbles or walking on wooden stilts, cut from the hedges or made from old cans with ropes attached, were more seasonal activities. Home-made catapults also went in and out of fashion. The young ones enjoyed playing 'tig', 'hide and seek' or just rolling tyres. The 'floor' of their playground was well bedded down by the break-time trains, lorries and cars that ran around issuing their various sounds and signals.

J.J. Doherty with his busman's cap, stick and wide tyre and well-mimicked sound of a large truck labouring on a steep hill seemed the most authentic driver in the yard. His facial contortions indicated beyond all reasonable doubt that a very serious operation was under way. Unmarked sprawling roots created traffic hazards and caused vehicles to break down. The Mistress provided a 'Road Recovery Service' consisting of a warm pat on the back and some words of reassurance.

Some juniors took the 'Long Piss' competitions, which were held at the back of the school, very seriously. A few competitors at a time would line up on the cinder hillock and let fly with full gusto. Some with higher aspirations and blessed with exceptional firing power stood on upturned buckets and attempted to send power hosings across the wall that separated the senior and junior grounds! Those of quieter disposition just stood transfixed as they marvelled at their frothy bubbles and the steam rising in the frosty air.

Occasionally, 'disagreements' would arise in the school yard and such matters would have to be settled in the 'ring' opposite Sunnybank Terrace at the top of the creamery brae on the way home. Word of an impending fight would spread like wildfire and a crowd would gather to watch the participants strip to their snake-buckled waists and 'square up' to one another. Occasionally one fighter, oozing self-confidence and therefore described as 'chan', might 'take on' two others. A nose pumping blood or a cry, 'the Master is coming', would usually terminate these bouts. We'd then scatter in all directions and have to settle for a less exciting but more regular vista – Janey Mc Caffrey at her door in 'Mudwall Row', killing time as she awaited Mickey's arrival, Quirkes tending to their aviary of beautiful birds, Tom 'Hugh D' filling in a pot-hole, a dilapidated van, topped with caged hens, taking off from Kearns's in a cloud of smoke, dust and feathers or ex-Garda Kyne (father of Desmond, the iconographer) stepping it out with sleek greyhounds by his side.

Keeping the school fires burning was a serious business. We got permission in turn to go up the 'Folly' (a narrow raised path with hedging on either side leading to a crab-tree plantation) before 'home- time' to gather 'cipini solais' for the following day. These twigs were placed on the dying embers to dry out. They would hiss and spit, often catch fire, resembling burning whins, and have to be quenched and left on the stone shelf along the hearth for relighting in the morning. We also had to bring in our ten-shilling notes per term, or an equivalent worth of turf to supplement the Department of Education's miserly £14 'Heating and Cleaning Grant' and thus keep Jack Frost at bay.

Sweeping and tidying up were other daily tasks. Before sweeping, we sprinkled water on the floor to keep down the dust. We also set off false alarms for poor spiders by scooping their webs with our hazel handled brooms of turkey feathers. These assignments, just like gathering the firewood, were not viewed as chores. Anything to get away from the lessons was considered something of a bonus.

Religion was an integral part of our daily programme with regular recitation of prayers, which we had to learn by heart. The language in some of these could be a little archaic and so we didn't always pick up the words correctly. One could identify with a poor fellow from Belturbet who was heard to say, 'Turn then most gracious apple-cake thine eyes of mercy towards us'!

The Irish 'Bible' at that time was called 'A Catechism of Catholic Doctrine', printed and bound in the Republic of Ireland, approved by the Archbishops and bishops of Ireland with its Imprimatur by +Joannes Carolus, Archiepiscopus Dublinensis, Hiberniae Primas, Dublini, die 2a mensis Februarii, anni 1951. It had 108 pages and cost the princely sum of one penny. The first 13 pages included Prayers, Chief Spiritual Works of Mercy, Eight Beatitudes, Mysteries of the Rosary and holy pictures. Then there were the Catechism questions and answers from No 1 (Who made the world?) to No.443 ('what are the principal ceremonies?') on page 103. The final section dealt with 'The manner of answering a priest at Mass'. By the time we had finished we were 'off by heart' experts on actual sin, mortal sin, venial sin, capital sins and sins that injured our neighbour's character ('rash judgement, calumny and detraction'). We knew what to do when tempted by impure thoughts and that 'everyone must belong to the Catholic Church and no one can be saved who, through his own fault, remains outside it'. We knew that presumption was 'a foolish expectation of salvation without making use of the means necessary to obtain it' and that God could see us 'for nothing is hidden from his all-seeing eyes'. We knew that souls had four possible destinations.

First and foremost there was Hell. It was a state designated for those who willingly 'with full knowledge and full consent' turned their back on God. Then there was Heaven above, the seat of the blest. The other two 'joints' were Purgatory and Limbo. They lay somewhere in between. Limbo was a place where the unbaptised were supposed to languish for eternity. More humane characters like St Thomas Aquinas suggested that it was a kind of kindergarten, a place of natural happiness for those who hadn't committed any personal sin. As far as we were concerned it had an interesting ring but that was all. We were glad it wasn't an option for we had all been taken to the church and baptized, even without our mothers, shortly after we arrived! Purgatory was a place or state of temporal punishment for those who still had a few venial sins on board and so needed a bit more cleansing before getting in above.

My favourite subject was History. I found the fables and stories relating to ancient Ireland particularly fascinating – the arrival of the Partholonians, how the Tuatha De Danann, a legendary race of superhuman heroes, who ousted the Fir Bolg at the battle of Moytura near Cong in Co. Mayo, lost their own power and control of the place to the Milesians and later re-emerged as fairies, the love affairs of Diarmaid and Grainne, of Niamh and Oisin and his sojourn in Tir na nOg (the land of Eternal Youth). We learned all about Fionn Mac Cumhaill and his powerful army, the Fianna that defended the High King, whose royal seat was on the Hill of Tara. Fionn himself operated from his main fortress on the Hill of Allen near Newbridge.

There were the great-sounding names of Giolla Deacair, the Tuatha De Danann magician, Caoilte Mac Ronáin, Fionn's nephew, Cormac Mac Airt, the High King and Goll Mac Morna, who led Clann Morna of Connaught. Then there was the most famous legend of them all, 'The Táin Bó Cuailnge', which recounted how Cúchulainn, the Hound of Ulster, single-handedly stopped Queen Medb's Connacht armies. That story included the great but sad battle between the famous warrior and his close friend, Ferdia. All came about because Queen Medbh wanted Daire Mac Fiachna's famous brown bull (the Donn Cuailnge) to rival her husband Ailill's great white fellow, Finnbeannach, and so outdo him in wealth. Despite advice from every quarter, she insisted on doing a 'Tony Blair/George Bush' on it, thus causing 'mass destruction'. Ferdia and Cúchulainn fought near Ardee for four days and there was still a stalemate. So Cúchulainn had to use his Gae-bolg to end the fight. He himself died of a broken heart some time later. These and all the other stories about the Children of Lir, Deirdre of the Sorrows, Fionn and the Salmon of Knowledge, Etain and Midir, the Three Sons of Turenn etc. opened up for me what Bryan Mac

Mahon would have called the windows of wonder. Most of the stories from the later periods in Irish history were tinged with sadness. King Brian Boru won the battle but lost his life. Dermot Mac Murrough wasn't happy until he landed the Normans on top of us. With Kinsale, it was a case of 'so near and yet so far'!

Still, Eoghan Ruadh O' Neill gave us a bit of a lift when he defeated Munroe's Scottish army at Benburb in 1646 and so too did another very popular hero, Patrick Sarsfield. With the help of 'Galloping Hogan' and a small band of men, he intercepted the train bringing ammunition to the Williamites, who were laying siege to the city of Limerick. He got through the enemy lines and blew up eighteen wagons. For ages after hearing this story, his famous statement, 'Sarsfield is the word and Sarsfield is the man', was bandied about in the school yard!

The English lessons were quite enjoyable despite the fact that conformity was the name of the game. Independent thought and creativity of expression in oral or written form weren't exactly encouraged. When we were supposed to know our poetry by heart, the Master would get us to stand within the frame of the door leading to the cloakroom and recite from there in front of the whole class. You could feel like a right 'eegit' encased in that position, especially if you made a 'hames' of it by getting your lines crossed, or coming to a full stop where there was only meant to be a comma.

Geography wasn't exactly the flavour of the time as it involved learning off 'reams of stuff' - the county towns of Ireland, the cotton towns of Yorkshire and just about every river, mountain and lake from Fair Head in Antrim to Mizen Head in Cork.

Preparing to serve on the altar was challenging, but at least it gave us the opportunity to taunt our sisters, who were banned from having such intimacy with the Lord. We had to learn off all the Latin responses and these didn't trip lightly off our West Cavan tongues. The novelty of it all got us through the 'Ad Deum qui laetificat', the 'saecula saeculorum' and 'sed libra nos a malo'. We just loved to outclass fellow servers as we thumped our chests at the 'mea culpa, mea culpa, 'mea maxima culpa' (and even had the audacity outside to change the sacred words to 'me a cow-boy, me a cow-boy , me a Mexican cow-boy') but when it came to the 'De profundis' that's where Aughrim was lost!

We did our bit for the foreign missions, distributing 'Africa' and Pudsy Ryan's 'Far East' across the village. We collected used stamps for the Mill Hill Fathers in Freshford, pricked holes in 'Rosary Cards' and kept the 'Black Baby' nodding appreciatively in response to our pennies.

As the end of our final year approached and our preparation for the two major events, Confirmation and the Primary Certificate Examination, began to 'heat up', others envied our new status. Even the Master himself seemed more benevolent, apart from the odd occasion when he sensed that we would self-destruct and leave his own reputation in tatters.

Confirmation, with its ill-founded fear of the Bishop's 'fierce clatter across the cheek', and promises of Wisdom, Understanding, Counsel, Fortitude, Knowledge, Piety and Fear of the Lord, came and went. Duly lubricated with 'oil of olives, mixed with balm and blessed by the priest on Holy Thursday', we were ready to freewheel as perfect Christians and soldiers of Jesus Christ!

The Primary Cert. also came and went. Like Confirmation, it heralded the end of childhood. A terminal test introduced in 1929, made compulsory in 1943 for all those in sixth class and finally abolished in 1967, it 'covered' three subjects; Arithmetic, English and Irish. All the emphasis back then was on numeracy and literacy. Each of the exams lasted one and a half hours.

There were two papers in Arithmetic and these covered problem solving, fractions, mental arithmetic and simple interest.

'A' consisted of 20 short question E.g.
If £1 =2.80 dollars, how many dollars should be got for £200?

'B' included 5 longer questions and you had to answer three of these.
E.g. In a 40 ton mixture of sand, gravel and cement, the sand weighs 24 tons 10cwts., and the gravel 10tons and 4cwts.
Find: (a) the weight of the cement and (b) what percentage of the mixture is cement?

There were two parts to the English paper.
You had to write a one page essay on a choice of subjects and answer some comprehension questions and a few others on basic grammar.

The subjects in 1958 were as follows:
- a   Wild Birds
- b   A dream you had
- c   You fell into the river and after much difficulty reached safety.
       Write a letter to your friend telling him (or her) all about it.
- d   Railways
- e   You fought with Brian Boru at Clontarf or with Sarsfield at Ballyneety. Describe your adventures and feelings on that occasion.

The layout of the Irish paper was quite similar to the English. The choice of compositions in 1958 was as follows:
- a   Daoine a thugann cuairt ar an scoil seo againne.
- b   Siucra
- c   Cleas a d'imir na scoláiri orm
- d   Agallamh (cómhra) idir faoilean (faoileog) agus londubh : gach éan a rá gur fearr a shaol féin ná saol an éin eile.

For many of us the most noteworthy feature of the Primary Certificate examination was its location rather than the exam itself. We had to sit it in the more modern Uragh Girls N.S. (built in 1899!). Here we were joined by other scholars from outlying schools at Commas, Altachullion and Tiercahan. Imagine being able to breath the same air, under the same roof, alongside the opposite sex at a time in life when they were becoming more attractive by the day! There we were, brimful of longing but rock-bottom in confidence, unable to relate to Dev's 'comely maidens' of the 40's and 50's! Within months, some of us would be whisked off to single-sex boarding schools where our sexual diet during term time would consist of a weekly mass- time glimpse of some female workers. Needless to say, this didn't exactly satisfy the sexual needs of testosterone-driven young males!

While there was something exciting about going away to a college boarding school at that time to study subjects such as Greek, Latin and Science, and it did open up pathways to secure and pensionable employment, it placed us in a kind of 'no man's land' where we were isolated from family, neighbours and the general interaction that was such an integral part of every small rural community. For a time at least, it loosened, if not severed, the knot that bound us to our native places.

Today Uragh Boys N.S. lies in ruins, its windows shattered, its yards overgrown with nettles and other weeds. There's no 'Folly' to be seen, no 'trains' letting off steam, no laurel jail, no marla, no smell of dust, chalk or fresh intestinal gas, no blackboard and easel, no maps hanging from spools, no sign of the 'Black Baby' or master's 'wand', just an eerie silence all round. Even the creamery, once nearby, has disappeared. The children have moved to a new, co-ed, centrally-heated school, conveniently situated closer to the village with modern playground equipment, televisions, white boards and coloured pens. There's tarmac to the front, back and sides. The old Master and Mistress, God rest and reward them, lie peacefully in Killaghaduff. Only the memories remain.

'The School Around the Corner's not the same'!

Rolling out the wire (Photo ESB archives)

Seeing the Light

The E.S.B. (Electricity Supply Board) was established on August 11, 1927, and became responsible for the generation, promotion, transmission, distribution and sale of electricity, but for Swanlinbar and other rural areas electrification was still a long way off. In fact, it wasn't until the late 30's and early 40's that the government and E.S.B. drew up plans for 'Rural Electrification'. Even then the war held things up so that people living in urban areas such as Lusk in North Dublin – not more than 20 miles from our capital city- in Skerries, Co. Dublin and Ballyshannon in Co. Donegal had to wait until the late 40's to get an E.S.B. connection.

The whole project, destined to bring about 'the greatest revolution in Irish rural life since the Land War of the late nineteenth and early twentieth centuries', would cost over £80 million from the time the first pole was erected in Kilsallaghan, Co. Dublin on November 5, 1946, until March 1976, by which time 420,000 rural households had been connected to the new network. Surveying in County Cavan (the last county in Ireland where this took place) didn't commence until 1948 when the ball was set rolling in Gowna. To day we tend to take the humble light bulb for granted, but it wasn't so back then when it breathed new life and changed the outlook, attitudes and living standards of those dwelling in the darkest pockets of our land.

I don't suppose ordinary folk ever realised the enormity of the task undertaken by the chief engineers, W.F. Roe and P.J.Dowling, and all their units scattered around the 792 areas within the 26,000 square miles of our fledgling State. One million poles had to be inspected, purchased, shipped from Finland, Norway and Sweden, skinned, creosoted, stored, transported by a fleet of tractors, often through narrow, winding roads and lanes, dragged through fields using horses and traces and then erected in holes that were four foot deep. Conductors, 100,000 transformers, 75,000 miles of wire and a host of other items, often in short supply, had to be found and connected up.

Before the arrival of electricity, people depended on candles and all kinds of lamps for artificial light. Splendid brass ones with decorative globes sometimes graced the parlour table, but the old Tilley seldom got past the kitchen where it issued its constant hiss in response to the odd pump. A Tilley with the brand name, 'Aladdin', was 'a cut above the others' with its white meshed mantle and tall delicate globe. The new mantle was white and pink and came in a see-through packet. It had a silky feel. The Aladdin's wick had to be trimmed and its globe regularly shined with newspapers. Great care had to be taken when lighting the mantle and replacing the globe as any jerky movement would cause it to disintegrate into dust particles. But when turned up, it gave a wonderful warm glow. With deft movements of wrist and hand close to the light, some could entertain us children by creating a zoo of shadowy animals on the walls and wooden ceiling of the room. When the Aladdin was turned down for the night or when it was time to go to bed, we had to grope our way upstairs in the dim candlelight, making sure not to drop the 'Wee Willie Winkle' holder on the way.

In 1941, Noel Coffey, a local entrepreneur, brought electricity to Swanlinbar. There were other 'Noel Coffeys' throughout the length and breath of Ireland – there were 140 privately owned schemes in the country as far back as 1922, but these were mostly based in urban areas - and many a one owes them a great deal of gratitude for using their expertise to brighten up people's lives before the E.S.B. arrived.

Noel's father, an auctioneer from the Brackley area, bought the old mill (that was listed on the Ordnance Survey map of 1833) and employed Benny Beacom, a highly experienced miller, to run it for him. Over the years water was stored in a dam up the Tanyard Lane, and flowed down the Mill Race to turn the great wheel that drove the turbines powering the corn mill. By the end of the 30's, the mill had become dilapidated and the equipment had fallen into a state of disrepair. Noel had it remodelled by an old style millwright called John Greene and proceeded to mill meal there from 1940 until 1952. Compulsory tillage during the war years ensured a plentiful supply of oats and so the mill flourished. Noel got a generator and installed light there. He also linked up two neighbours, local teacher, Joe Connaughton and Mrs. Clarke, the publican, to his new system. Candles became scarce and paraffin was next to impossible to get during the war years. Not surprising, he was inundated with requests for light. So, he sought a permit to install a commercial system in the town and this was granted. Fortunately, he was able to get a supply of surplus wire and generators from Poulaphouca and suitable poles from a nearby wood. With the help of Joe Beacom, Benny's son, he trimmed these and preserved them with creosote.

Mickey Gilbride took on the contract of erecting them with the aid of pick-axe, spade and shovel at a rate of ten-shillings per pole. They 'covered' a wide area including Main Street, Chapel Square, Mill Street and the Church Road. So, while Adolf was switching off the lights in London, Noel was brightening up the homesteads of Swad!

Before Christmas each year, Harry Toal, a local general trader and fowl dealer, paid a little extra to have light 'late into the night' for plucking turkeys and geese. Also, if there was a late-night dance or concert in the village, a similar arrangement was made to extend the service beyond the usual 12.30a.m. deadline and all the other citizens benefited at no extra charge. The farmers got their meal by day and Swad had its light by night.

In the early days, Noel had no meters so the monthly charge was based on the number of light sockets installed. Needless to say, these were kept to a minimum by the thrifty townsfolk. In the mid 1940's, when the Electricity Board in Northern Ireland was upgrading its equipment, Noel bought a supply of their meters and installed these. From then on, payment was based on usage.

The water for all milling operations came from the 'Mill Dam'. It flowed rapidly down the 'Mill Race' and turned the huge wooden wheel alongside the mill. Terrified that the water would run short, Noel purchased a diesel engine to supplement his supply. Sometimes, while people slept peacefully in their beds, he had to smuggle fuel from the North to keep it topped up. He had many 'narrow shaves' with the Customs and was eventually caught. As a result, he lost his oil licence for a time and only had it restored when he convinced the authorities that every small farmer would be left in a state of destitution if he could no longer grind their corn! He had to

Noel Coffey, the man who first brought electricity to Swad.
Photo: Anne Coffey

come up with innovative ways of hiding his 'illicit' oil. Hugh Cullen's petrol tanks, empty during the war years, proved to be a real God send.

In January 1950 the Parish Council, under the chairmanship of Rev. Canon Michael Kelly, met to see if people were interested in bringing rural electrification to Swad. Members were appointed to canvass householders in town and country to ascertain the approximate number willing to install the light. A month later they reported that the overall response was very positive and so hopes were high that the project might get off the ground before the end of the year. However, when 'a few bucks from the E.S.B.' conducted their own survey to establish who in the area classified as 'Bawnboy' (which included Swanlinbar) wanted to 'get in the light', the response was not quite as good. A hold-up was inevitable. The data entered on their report makes for interesting reading and was as follows:

Square Miles – 32.9   Total houses on map – 748
Economic Acceptance – 379   Uneconomic Acceptance – 105
Refusal – 246   Doubtful – 47
Vacant and not seen – 76   (ESB Archives)

Some country folk expressed reservations. They didn't like the idea of having poles erected on their land and were afraid that crops might be damaged while this work was going on. Not knowing anything about the new power, they thought they might be electrocuted or that once installed, the Board might 'up the price'. The 'fixed charge' was a major issue. The idea of having to pay it for a lifetime wasn't very palatable. So quite a few would have agreed with the old bachelor who declared, 'by my sowl, I'd as lief (rather) stay the way I am'!

However, in the heel of the reel, after much encouragement from Canon Kelly and some little persuasion from the 'Area Organiser', who was specially trained to promote acceptance by demonstrating the special benefits, many of the 'initially-reluctant' gave in and the majority signed on.

By November 1952 creosoted poles were being deposited in strategic piles around the place and power lines were being mapped out. Labourers were employed to dig the holes at a rate of one shilling and ten and a half pence per hour for a 48 hour week. The poles were drawn by horses and a team of six men placed them in position. Then it was time for the 'wire men' to get down to work (or rather up to work!). Within a matter of three months, forty men – all but 18 of whom were from the locality – had everything in place. The 'Anglo Celt' of March 14, 1953, announced that the E.S.B. current would be switched on at 5p.m. in St. Mary's Hall on Tuesday, March 17, 1953. This was to be followed by a dance. 'A night of nights' was expected.

The official 'switch on' for 500 houses in the 25 square mile area embracing Swanlinbar, Bawnboy and Templeport was carried out by Fr. Murtagh P.P., who noted that the event 'synchronised with the feast of the National Apostle, who brought the light of faith to the country'. Fr. Tully C.C. Bawnboy, a man renowned for his wit, reminded the locals that they would now be getting their electricity from water and not from Coffey! The attendance also included former Kinawley P.P., Very Rev. M. Canon Kelly P.P. V.F. Ballinamore – who with Fr. Tully started the movement to have electricity brought to the area - Rev. T.J. Brennan C.C., Rev. Mr. Colvin, The Manse, Swanlinbar, Messers. F. Mc Govern and J. Connaughton, joint secretaries, Swanlinbar Parish Council, as well as officials and engineers from the E.S.B. The Church of Ireland minister, Rev. John Richard Wheelock, was unavoidably absent. Other Parish Council members present included Messers P. Woods (Vice-Chairman), J. Carr, P. Lunney, B. Mc Govern, S. Young, H. Cullen, P. Prior, P.J. Mc Hugh, G. Mc Govern, T. Greene, F. Mc Teigue, P. Mc Govern P.C., F.J. Mc Govern and Dr. J. V. Mc Loughlin.

In the beginning people out the country were all agog at the power of electricity and the whole talk was about 'units' and the 'fixed charge'. Some were afraid that they might not be able to afford to keep it, and so opted initially for one or maybe two bulbs and a socket for the wireless. In some cases too, only the man of the house was allowed to switch on the light as they were afraid that the house could be burned down or that you could be electrocuted if you weren't careful enough. Still, they were delighted to forget about wet batteries and know that they would no longer have to spend time cleaning globes. The only real draw-back was the fact that it spoiled the glow in the fire! Before long, country folk were talking about plugs, fuses, watt bulbs and earth wires as if referring to a 'mug of tae'! As was the case in other rural parts, locals weren't content with light alone or indeed with the wireless. They opted for a host of appliances that really took the drudgery out of life. These in order of preference (according to E.S.B. records) were as follows:

1 Radio sets 4 Cookers 7 Washing machines
2 Irons 5 Vacuum cleaners 8 Water heaters
3 Kettles 6 Fires 9 Refrigerators

(ESB Archives)

Erecting the pole (Photo ESB archives)

Wirelesses on sale at that time included the Murphy, Pye, Philips, Bush, S.E.C., Mullard and H.M.V.

In 1952, the E.S.B. 'bought Noel out' but asked him to continue to offer his supply until such time as they became fully operational. He then sold his mill. Most of the beautiful cut stone from the building was ground into gravel and used to make concrete for the foundations of the local Garda barracks, all in the name of progress! How builders today would value those stones. A few years later, Noel, who always harboured a desire to travel, set off with his family to Canada. Sadly, his contribution to the quality of life in the village went unsung. He was an entrepreneur well ahead of his time. A self-taught man and a great community person, he looked for no 'hand-outs'. He saw a niche for himself in the market and filled it to the best of his ability.

Noel and his family returned from Canada in 1968 and set up a T.V., radio and electrical shop in Belturbet. When I interviewed him there a few years ago, he really entertained me with his anecdotes. For example, he recalled a notable visit to Harry Toal, one of Swad's great characters. Noel wanted to collect payment for his supply but unfortunately, his light was rather dim on the particular night in question. On hearing about his errand, Harry summoned his wife and in his great Armagh accent ordered her to light a candle, or bring a box of lights quickly so that he could count the money 'to furnish Mr. Coffey with payment for his light'! Shortly after he came back from abroad, a rural farmer, fed up with payments to the E.S.B., came up to him, expressed delight at his return, announced that he had a small lake 'out the back' and wondered if he would do him a favour and 'take the electricity out of it, the way he did in Swad'.

But time marched on. The E.S.B. with its high-powered supply brought salesmen with their 'Vacuum-Masters' that could dry hair, hoover up the dust, perfume the whole place and the 'divil knows what'. Corners that never saw the light of day had to get a lick of paint. Ghost stories lost their appeal. In 1955 Burke-Clancy and Co. from Galway brought running water to the village. Some time later a sewage scheme was in place. With light to guide, you could now lighten your load upon a throne and walk away contented! No more than the oil lamp and the lantern, the dock under the blue sky and newspaper strips in the outside unit became redundant! Life changed.

On top of the world! (Photo ESB archives)

Aunty Kathleen

AUNTY KATHLEEN

Listening and sharing, you were everyone's friend,
You trusted in God right to the end.
Nodding by the fire, relaxing with a prayer,
Taking some time to stand and stare.
Patting a dog, admiring a flower
You never aspired to wealth or power.
Many of us learn far too late,
That they serve too who sit and wait.

Aunty Kathleen, my father's sister, was a rotund, jolly lady, who lived to the ripe old age of ninety one. That was in keeping with the old Irish proverb, 'maireann croí eadrom í bhfad' (A light heart lives long). She had many of the great qualities we associate with women of her time - was deeply religious, unwavering in her faith and trust in God, good humoured, generous and selfless to an extreme. Mass was the focal point of her day and on her way home afterwards, she brought the newspapers to the housebound in the village. She was always on hand to help anyone in need and laid out 'half the parish'. She had a well-worn prayer book, laden with memorial cards, novenas and special prayers that had to be said for a particular length of time or at a specific hour of the day, dried petals, holy pictures – some with relics attached – and all held together with an elastic band.

For many years she did the station to the Holy Well at Oughteragh in Ballinamore and went on pilgrimages to Lough Derg and Knock. Once, she got a bit of a legacy and fulfilled a life-long ambition to visit Lourdes. She returned laden with statues and statuettes, snowy water-grottoes, holy pictures of every saint that ever trampled this planet and medals for the whole country. For a time, her kitchen table resembled a mini conveyor belt as tiny bottles of holy water were assembled in military formation, filled from a large container and labelled for dispersion!

Talking about pilgrimages, one very memorable trip to Knock at a later stage comes to mind. It was at the time that Monsignor Horan was transforming the shrine and had the parking section cordoned off with wire fencing. I hardly had the car switched off when Aunty Kathleen, with her insatiable appetite for prayer, disembarked and made a bee-line for the church. Unfortunately, she didn't see the fence and before you could say Jack Robinson her eleven stone frame was impaled. So there she was, bobbing up and down in the Mayo breeze. I terminated her brief moment of apparent levitation, engineering her extraction as quickly as I could. Fortunately, her layers of cardigans and jumpers cushioned her and saved her from inevitable puncture and she was ready to "take the field" again in next to no time.

Because of her anxiety to do the right thing, she could be rather scrupulous and would cycle off posthaste on her 'High Nellie' to the Graan monastery near Enniskillen whenever she sensed that she had overdone the gossip and needed to wipe the slate clean and make a fresh start.

Aunty Kathleen with her 'High Nellie'

Kathleen and a few of her strategically placed friends had the village well 'covered'. They held council in a huddle before and after the 8.30a.m. Mass and continued at various locations later in the day. They focused on local rather than international events and crises, on Father Mallon rather than Joseph Stalin. They had an absolute 'field day' and would go 'ninety to the dozen' whenever a priest died or was due to be transferred. Speculation regarding his possible successor was then the number one item on their agenda. For weeks before the annual priests' retreat, rumours abounded and the 'Anglo Celt' was anxiously awaited for news of the bishop's appointments. Once the name was announced, Scotland Yard wouldn't have a look in! Every possible source was tapped and soon an identikit emerged. Jewels such as the following began to circulate – 'was fond of money', 'had no time for publicans', 'you wouldn't know what to make of him', 'keeps you all day at mass', 'a saintly man', 'fond of the drop', 'doesn't get on so well with the other priests', 'comes from somewhere in Leitrim'! Any fresh crumb of knowledge with regard to the proposed incumbent gave the holder a special status at the morning conclave near the church door. The temptation to embellish any fleshless facts must have been irresistible.

Some priests frowned on the local newscasters or 'chin-wags'. Conscious that careless talk, based on assumption and hearsay, could damage reputations if not assassinate character, priests took the odd swipe at them from the altar, but in retrospect this was probably somewhat unfair and failed to acknowledge the fact that news was the lifeblood of the people. Besides, the whole business was quite harmless. An interest in others was at its core. Apart from their adding a certain spice to humdrum living and ensuring that the whole village didn't nod off, many a need might have gone unnoticed but for their vigilance. They also preserved what Bryan Mac Mahon would have called the 'social equipoise' – raised the lowly and called the haughty to heel. Thankfully, just when they were becoming an endangered species, they got a timely boost when psychologists discovered that gossip is good for your health and can add years to your life!

Kathleen was also unbelievably superstitious. Dropping a knife, fork, or dishcloth etc., breaking a mirror, opening an umbrella indoors, viewing the new moon for the first time through glass, placing a shoe on the table, or walking under a ladder sent alarm bells ringing. So too did the sight of a lone magpie. She taught me the popular rhyme about that bird – 'One for sorrow; two for joy; three for a wedding; four for a boy; five for silver; six for gold; and seven for a secret never to be told.' She nearly died when I bought a green car because of this colour's association with the fairies, but was somewhat relieved when she heard that its registration number included two sevens! She was convinced that seeing a black cat or white horse, touching wood, crossing fingers, finding a four-leaved clover or a rabbit's foot or nailing an iron horse-shoe to a door could 'turn the tide' in your favour! If you spilt salt, you had to throw some over your left shoulder to 'blind the devil' and thus counteract the bad luck!

When her only child, Frank, died shortly after birth in the National Maternity Hospital in Holles Street, Dublin in 1950, Aunty Kathleen bore this cross with   fortitude and began to treat me, her six year old nephew, as one of her own. I visited her daily and with the eyes of a child got to know her every move. Her whereabouts were quite predictable. She was usually in residence, doing a myriad of household chores such as cleaning her range, tidying out drawers or tightening a handle with her 'turnscrew', washing down her soot-stained ceiling, getting Uncle Frank's tea, praying or dozing in front of the fire, entertaining some guest or else up the town or out the back having a chin-wag with her neighbour, Sally, on her way back from emptying her po (chamber pot) or bringing in fuel. In or out, her door was always on the latch and I enjoyed slipping in quietly and 'getting her on the hop'. She would give a jump, raise her arms, tighten them, throw her eyes to Heaven and on seeing me would exclaim, 'O Sacred Heart of Jesus', or 'Bad scran to you for making me heart go crossways!' She always had a big penny tucked away in her apron pocket and presented it to me like a sacred host with the stipulation that I was to keep my silence.

She was renowned for her hospitality. Hers, like that of many others at the time, was a 'key in the door' house and certainly not one of those 'Here's your hat, what's your hurry' establishments! 'Wilya' didn't feature in her vocabulary. There was absolutely no point in telling her that you were 'only rising from the table'. Everyone who called simply had to have the cup o' 'tay' (on which you could certainly 'trot a mouse') and a thick hunk of her boiled porter cake or fresh soda bread, well capped with Killeshandra butter. Her visitors brought ginger cake, fig rolls, tea cakes, or some real free range eggs carefully wrapped in the 'Celt'. Around Christmas time, they might arrive with slabs of Chester cake. They exchanged gossip and read 'Willow Pattern' cups, or blue and white striped mugs while resting their weary limbs alongside the hearth. The odd very special client might get a liberal non-drinker's measure of the 'creatur'!

Some of her more regular visitors had their own unofficial times and she became worried about their welfare whenever they failed to turn up on schedule. No one was ever expected to account for his or her visit. Presence was all that mattered.

Frequently off-duty guards or customs men, stationed far from home, dropped in for a chat, or simply to while away the time snoozing comfortably in front of her well-stoked range or listening to Philip Greene giving his commentary on her Pye wireless.

I knew from experience that there were some occasions when she preferred to be alone – to listen to Mrs. Dale's Diary or the Kennedys of Castlerosse or prepare her husband's tea, or tend to his needs when he would arrive home on his bicycle after a hard day's work as the local tradesman.

Her canine friends were just as welcome as her human visitors. No 'Bran','Topsy', 'Prince', 'Spot', 'Shep' or 'Fido' ever left her doorway hungry. No wonder they always tailed her as she went on her errands.

She had a one-legged kitchen table. This was attached to an iron bar that ran horizontally along the wall, thus allowing the table with its foldable leg to be placed close to her fire or elsewhere depending on the weather or need. When not in use, it could be lifted up against the wall; an ingenious idea for that time, I thought.

Monday was wash day in St. Aidan's and this was something to behold! In those days there were no front-loaders with digital jet and aqua-cycle systems, nor any time and delay starts and child safety features. Arms bared to the neck, Aunty Kathleen would set up her naval-shaped galvanized bath-pan with its scrubbing board on two backless kitchen chairs, fill it with steaming hot water, grab the Sunlight soap or Rinso (with Rickett's Blue close by) and go head-to-head with any 'skid' marks on my uncle's drawers – but not before 'Whiskers', her sleek black cat, anticipating a storm ahead would have scrambled from the kitchen. Of course, all items would have been left to steep overnight Soon you'd have a crescendo of scrubbing and squeezing , great navy bloomers would be in full-blown sail and huge Atlantic breakers would be rolling ashore near range and door!

I usually viewed proceedings from the safety of my perch on her kitchen side-board. This was not her favourite time for receiving visitors. 'Oh dear, who's that at the door?' she would cry if she heard the slightest rattle in her hallway. Fortunately, anyone who did come usually took one look, promised to come back later and made a hasty exit! The action-filled ritual continued for an hour or more with Uncle Frank's shirt collars getting the Robin Starch treatment along the way.

Then it was time to wring and hang out to dry. Later on in the evening, with the help of her old Tailor's Goose, that normally sat patiently beside her singing kettle on her neat black-leaded range, she hammered the whole lot into shape and proudly carried the neatly folded garments to their cupboard upstairs.

Around Halloween, when large potatoes were plentiful, she took to making boxty. Some spuds were peeled and boiled, others were peeled, grated and squeezed in a muslin bag to remove water and starch and then rolled together with flour into cakes that bubbled away on top of cutlery in a huge saucepan. When they were ready, she made cornflour sauce, and with this and a knob of butter on top of the Boxty, we let our ears back and together 'horsed' into a ferocious feed. Later on, the remaining cakes were sliced and fried. Taken with a few cuts of hairy bacon (ie.with bristle attached), the lot would put hair on anyone's chest! Of course, she had several other dishes with odd names such as 'Colcannon', 'Brusey', 'Inge-buck', 'Stir-a-bout' and others still 'on the go' today such as Sago, Tapioca and Semolina. If her larder was low, she'd 'stick on' a few slices of bread and fry them in lard or dripping or heat up some bread and milk in a saucepan and serve it with a generous topping of sugar.

When it came to taking precautions against the demon Constipation, my aunt was a great believer in such products as Glauber and Epsom salts, Milk of Magnesia, Andrew's Liver salts and of course that other old tried and proven antidote, overnight-steeped prunes. Any admonition attributed to the local medical practitioner, such as the one emphasising the need to 'let your wind blow freely' was reverently acknowledged and, much to our simple amusement, adherence to his advice was evidenced on occasions!

Whenever we saw Aunty Kathleen 'freewheeling' around our back, we knew she had some tit-bit on board. We would be encouraged to go out and play 'like good children'. We would feign obedience and listen within earshot for the latest. This often centred on someone who had or was about to have a B-A-B-Y – which she spelt out quietly for my mother's ears. Sometimes she would present some paraphernalia from an American parcel for my mother's perusal and sing the praises of the figure-enhancing Yankee corset. Then she was off out the door like a lamplighter– it had to be the one she entered!– with her usual parting refrain, 'That's all the news. It's time I was on my way'. Nothing remained but the whiff of the white camphor balls lodged in the American clothes.

Aunty Kathleen maintained her concern for others and sense of fun right to the end, long after a walking-frame replaced her High Nellie. She was born in Swanlinbar on May 4, 1909, was christened Catherine Mary Prior shortly afterwards and departed this world on March 26, 2001. I'm sure she found Heaven's door ajar. An té a bhíos fial roinneann Dia leis (God shares with the person who is generous).

St. Mary's Church. Built in 1828, it was renovated and rededicated in 1959.

THE CHURCH

Our lives revolved around the Church from the pouring on of baptismal water in St. Mary's to the thud of the black clay in Killaghaduff cemetery. During the intervening period, her priests were always on hand to offer solace and consolation in times of sickness or tragedy, tend to our spiritual needs, keep us 'on the straight and narrow' and save us from the devil's 'cloven hoofs'. Even the dogs in the street were not exempt from the Church's influence. When 'Cissie Mac of the Chapel Gates' rang the Angelus bell at twelve noon and six in the evening, all the dogs around, both 'Prod' and 'Papist' – and most were of dubious lineage – got a certain impulse to spring to life, assemble in Main Street and in unison bark out their ecumenical chant!

Being a good Catholic in those days was a full-time occupation. It involved Mass and Benediction on Sundays and Holy days, devotions to the Virgin Mary, family prayer, especially the Rosary and its 'Trimmings' (prayers for the canonization of Blessed Oliver and Martin de Porres, for the conversion of Russia and the fall of Communism, prayers to preserve us from 'pestilence, fire, lightning and tempest', for a sick calf or dying neighbour, the repose of a soul, a special intention, a happy death etc.); saying the 'Morning Offering' as well as the 'Angel of God' at night, making Holy Hours, 'Stations of the Cross' and renewing Baptismal vows, monthly confession of sins, recitation of the Angelus twice daily, wearing St. Philomena's cord, brown, green or blue scapulars and Miraculous medals, making visits to the church, church grounds and graveyard to gain indulgences at specific times, lighting penny candles, blessing yourself with Holy Water, saying three Hail Marys for the virtue of Holy Purity, making St. Brigid's crosses, giving up sweets or mortifying yourself in some other way during Lent, blessing yourself when going past a church, cemetery or funeral procession, making a public declaration of faith on Corpus Christi, supporting the clergy with dues and offerings, contributing to the foreign missions with donations to the 'Black Babies' or subscribing to periodicals such as 'The Far East', 'The Sacred Heart Messenger', 'Africa', 'Blessed Martin magazine', the 'Imeldist' and the 'The Word', reading these and other books such as those produced by the Catholic Truth Society or newspapers such as the 'Irish Catholic', attending Missions and Novenas, having Mass cards signed for relatives and friends, joining groups like the Knights of Columbanus, St. Vincent de Paul Society, Children of Mary, Legion of Mary, Sacred Heart Sodality or a Confraternity, Pioneer Total Abstinence Association and Apostolic Society, making novenas and saying special prayers e.g. the Thirty Days' Prayer and ejaculations, putting inordinate pressure on certain intermediary saints (e.g. St. Anthony for lost objects or St. Jude for lost causes) to 'storm Heaven'('intercede' was the big word we used!) in order to obtain special favours, going on pilgrimage to Knock, Croagh Patrick, Lough Derg, Fatima, Lourdes and various Holy wells. Of course it involved obeying all the other

Commandments of God and of His Church not referred to above. Each home was blessed and consecrated to the Sacred Heart. A small lamp glowed beneath His picture in the kitchen and we marvelled at the way He could keep us under constant surveillance irrespective of where we sat or stood! House Stations were held twice a year in many dioceses in Ireland but not in ours.

The vast majority of parishioners had an unquestioning faith and a great desire to hand this on intact to their children. They looked to the clergy for leadership and they in turn responded by giving clear and definite rulings about the rights and wrongs of most human issues. The laity may not have found their judgements particularly palatable at times, but at least they knew where they stood. Occasionally, they may have criticised the priest, but deep down they had the utmost respect, tinged with fear, for the 'cloth' and 'collar' and felt inadequate whenever an occasion arose where they had to keep 'His Reverence' in chat.

Nobody wanted to be 'read from from the altar' for some misdemenour or be subjected to the 'priestly curse' through which you could be struck dumb or might never again do any good. Their somewhat ambivalent attitude comes across in the old saying, ' Always keep out from the priests; that way you will always keep in with them'.

The priest was seen as the 'top dog' in the parish, well ahead of the local doctor or head teacher and always addressed as 'Father'. Men doffed their caps and saluted while women lowered their heads in deference to him. His exceptional power was well acknowledged. Whoever made the 'Nine Fridays' would not die unrepentant, but having the priest at your bedside as you breathed your last was considered the ultimate in terms of final comfort. Certain priests built up a reputation for having 'a good office', and people came from far and near to seek their prayers for special intentions.

The P.P. was a 'cut above' his assistants. He had greater security of tenure in the parish and commanded half the takings as opposed to the curates, who had to settle for a quarter apiece and could be moved at short notice by the bishop. People were conscious that over the years their ancestors had made tremendous sacrifices to build churches worthy of their God, and had taken pride in giving their priests great houses, comparable to those of the landlord classes. Most were happy to continue that tradition.

Mothers in particular were instrumental in keeping the faith alive in the home. They prayed fervently that a son or daughter might enter the 'service of God' and many did. Their joy was captured in the following lines, frequently quoted on Ordination cards at the time.

'But oh! To see you with the chalice
In vestments pure and white,
Dear Lord, that would be Heaven
To an Irish Mother's sight.'

During the course of twenty to twenty five years, fifteen priests, ten nuns and five Brothers from our parish alone 'went on the missions' to such far-flung regions as Nigeria, Ghana, Basutoland, U.S.A., Britain, India, South Africa and South America or else worked for the Lord in the home dioceses. When you multiply this by the number of similar parishes throughout the length and breadth of Ireland, you begin to get some idea of the enormous and selfless contribution made by Irish priests and religious at home and abroad over the years. In the past one hundred years 800 have died abroad. More than 50 of these died violently, thus becoming modern martyrs.

Eras in the past were often identified by reference to the tenure of a particular priest. Someone might remark, 'That was in Canon Kelly's time'. In actual fact, the degree of freedom and ease enjoyed in the parish was determined by the priest in charge. Hence such statements as, 'He wouldn't get away with that if Fr. Brennan (C.C. from 1947 to 1954) was still around!' The same reverend gentleman was a stern, awesome, bespectacled figure in biretta and soutane. He certainly didn't suffer fools easily and established a reputation for putting the 'fear of God' in his altar servers. Tall and thin and tight-skinned, he once made a swipe at a fellow with his breviary, but fortunately the lad 'ducked' and the holy book, after spreading an autumnal shower of enclosed leaflets in all directions, crashed into the sanctuary wall. He didn't 'put a tooth' in anything when he spoke from the altar, but most agreed that his bark was worse than his bite. He was a tireless worker, instrumental in building St. Mary's Hall, which opened in March 1951, organized very popular dances and brought top-class musical artists from all over the country to take part in his concerts. He certainly gave a great fillip to the social and cultural life of the parish.

Canon Kelly had a certain aura, showed great concern for the general welfare of his flock and was highly respected. I didn't serve on the altar during his tenure and so never had a chance to view him at close quarters.

Fr. John Murtagh (d.1955) was a jovial little country man, partial to the odd tipple or hot toddy and was barely visible behind the steering wheel of his ID 6709 Morris Minor. He arrived in the school one day when Lucy had her gander up and I was getting 'down the banks' and an 'odious leathering' to boot. But for his timely intervention ('what's happening to this poor young man?'), I was a 'gonner'! Poor Lucy got an awful 'gunk'! He loved his pipe and whenever he called to our house, he'd tap it on the range before restoking. Then he'd lie back in the chair and really make himself at home. I once heard him tell my father how he'd love to shoot a certain parishioner with a crooked sixpence. I thought it a terrible thing for a priest to say but wondered to myself how exactly he might carry it out!

The absent-minded, short-sighted Fr. Edward Fox was a musical, scientific and mathematical genius but he didn't get much of an outlet for his many talents during his long tenure in Swad. He did, however, assemble his own piano and sometimes got quite absorbed in this and in his various contraptions and inventions. He attracted great crowds to his bingo sessions in St. Mary's Hall and these raised much needed funds for parochial purposes. He had a nice easy way and we loved him.

Canon Thomas O' Dowd (d.1960) was quiet and unassuming, revered by all and never 'rocked the boat' while Canon Charles Matthews (d.1963) appeared to be something of a mystic. A generous, saintly man, his focus was always on the world to come and but for the intervention of his guardian angel, who worked overtime on his behalf, he could have entered it well before his time. He never bothered any of his mirrors as he reversed in a cloud of smoke out of the Chapel Square! He was the only man I knew who could pass up and down by the Customs hut without as much as a salute!

The Bishop visited the parish at Confirmation time and generally carried out something of an audit or thorough investigation of parochial affairs. While the occasion was marked by a celebratory, communal meal, one got the impression that the P.P's were quite pleased to see him off the premises. He issued his Pastoral letter during Lent. In this he usually warned about various things such as drink, company keeping, dances (real occasions of sexual sin) and dangerous literature. Pursuing pleasure usually got the 'thumbs down'. Sex was out of bounds unless within marriage and for the procreation of children. Dancing after midnight in the Kilmore diocese was just not on.

Confession on the first Thursday or Saturday of each month encouraged us to take stock on a regular basis and thus maintain our respect for God, man and the laws of our land. In this way it helped to curb unsocial behaviour and maintain a certain moral balance and order. Its demise is in tandem with a decline in our sense of wrong doing. Back then, crime was 'an unexpected, abnormal event', but as Garland pointed out in 1996, 'it has now become a routine part of modern-consciousness, an everyday risk.' The very fact that the Garda recorded 12,231 indictable offences in 1951 compared to 101,659 in 2005 tells its own story.

While Confession may have lifted a heavy weight off your shoulders – your slate was wiped clean and you were ready to make a fresh start – there was a certain downside to the ritual. You had to go through an 'Examination of Conscience', a whole check-list of 'shoulds' and 'shouldn'ts' suggested by teacher - Did I curse or take the name of the Lord, my God, in vain? Did I tell lies? Did I fight with my brothers or sisters? Did I forget to say my prayers or not do what I was told? Did I take what didn't belong to me? . . . Impure thoughts and actions were added to the catalogue at a later stage. To make matters worse, you might find yourself wedged in between a few oul ones muttering prayers or ejaculations or even talking to themselves. Then you could easily forget sins and all, and there'd be no one 'within an ass's roar' to give you a jump start with the 'Bless me, Father' bit. Once inside the dark confessional with its dusty kneeler and arm ledge, you had to make a special effort not to listen to what was being whispered on the far side.

Soon the priest would slide across the shutter, his silhouetted figure would appear behind the grill and you were on! As if that wasn't enough there was one particular priest who used to drawl out 'anything else, my child' whenever you paused. This put you under tremendous pressure to rattle off everything as quickly as you could and assure him right away that he had heard the lot. Otherwise, those outside would conclude that you were the very devil incarnate and have a good 'gawk' at you on the way out. If you were lucky, you would get 'Three Hail Marys' but if you had a big rigmarole of stuff to tell, you might be asked to say two decades of the Rosary! One way or another, you'd be glad to hear the 'Ego te absolvo'. Then you'd have to go through your fingers like the fires of Hell, or else expose your sinfulness and listen to the jibes of your mates. You'd be afraid not to say your penance before leaving the church in case you'd be knocked down on the way home and have to spend the rest of your days with the boyos down below.

Advance purification of body – getting a good scrub from head to toe in the bath-tub in front of the fire - was another integral part of the Saturday routine. As well as this, shoes had to be polished and our best gear had to be left ready for the morning. Then all roads led to St.

Mary's Church for no one would dream of missing Sunday Mass. It was part of the texture of life. Besides, what would the neighbours think or say if you failed to turn up? If you wanted to get a decent seat, it was imperative to get there in good time, well ahead of the crowd that chatted away amicably as they held up the houses in Chapel Square and eyed everyone who passed! We usually took a short 'cut' – turned left at Cassidy's Bar and Grocery, went down Pudding Lane and then slipped in by the back entrance.

In our house, Sunday, the rest day of the week, was more or less 'given over' to Mass, dinner, the Sunday newspapers (sold by Detta and Claire from behind Hackett's half-opened door) with their fashion and crossword competitions, Micheál Ó' Hehir, a walk down the road or along the river bank, a match or 'kick about' in Mac's field, Benediction, school lessons, Sean Og O' Ceallaghan's round up of Sports Results (first presented by him in 1938) and the Thomas Davis Lectures (first series of which was broadcast on September 27, 1953). No one back then engaged in any unnecessary servile work on a Sunday. It was forbidden by Church law and this was only relaxed in inclement weather if crops were in danger of being lost.

The Mass was in Latin. At that time, its sacrificial dimension was emphasized and there was little or no acknowledgement of the 'meal' aspect. The priest kept his back to the people and celebrated for them rather than with them. They rose and stood, knelt and sat as required. Very often they said the Rosary or murmured some other prayers and let him 'get on with it'. All this changed after the second Vatican Council (1962 – 1965). So too did our concept of God. Early on, I saw him as a great judge, with a long white beard, sitting on a throne above the clouds. He was usually surrounded by hosts of winged angels, all clad in white garments, playing harps and singing His praises. He kept a massive black notebook containing his rules and regulations. In this, he recorded our sins and misdemeanours and seemed to take a certain pleasure in writing them all down. Even before we got going at all, we were in trouble as a result of Adam taking that fatal bite of the apple in the Garden of Eden.

God was constantly in touch with the bearded St. Peter, who resided in a small gatehouse alongside the entrance to Heaven. He was a kind of Customs and Excise officer who checked with the Lord to see what kind of sins you had on board. If given the 'go ahead', Peter, still robed like a Pope, always dangling his keys and known affectionately as 'The Rock', opened the pearly gates, let you in, stamped your book, got one of the angels to measure you for a set of wings and show you to your place. Otherwise, a trap door opened and you landed in Purgatory or fell headlong into the roaring fires of Hell!

Like ancient Gaul, the church was divided into three main parts. There was the Sanctuary, which was 'cut off' from the rest by means of a railing, the central body with seats for men on the right and women on the left and a balcony, known as the 'Gallery' at the back. The choir operated from a small curtained off apartment above the women's section. Ranged around the local school mistress at the organ, it belted out 'Sweet Sacrament Divine', 'Sweet Heart of Jesus', 'Hail Queen of Heaven', 'The Bells of the Angelus', 'To Jesus's Heart All Burning', 'Faith of Our Fathers' etc. Occasionally the odd inquisitive member, whose mind might wander far from 'the panting heart of Rome', would succumb to temptation and peep out from behind the curtain to view the talent below!

When we were young, we generally went up on the 'Gallery', the only unisex centre in town. Here you could sit as a family in your own little pew and get a bird's eye view of the proceedings. Below, some women had their heads covered with mantillas - lace triangles, usually black and held in place by brown plastic-coated wire clips. Others had coloured scarves depicting hunting scenes or distracting views of exotic faraway places such as Manhattan, Piccadilly or the Eiffel Tower in Paris. Many of the younger girls wore theirs Grace Kelly style – crossed under the chin and tied at the back. The older women, who tended to dress in black, wore hats that were held in place with fancy pins. You might also espy the odd camel coat. On the right hand side, you could see a myriad of bald heads (most shiny and some carbuncled) and a scatter of caps on the sloping window sills alongside them. The children took their places in the front rows.

If you had fasted from midnight, were in the 'state of grace' (i.e. free from mortal sin) and had 'the right intention', you could go to Holy Communion. The drive to the rails was usually led by a few holy women near the front, while members of the choir, mostly impish girls feigning shyness and smelling of 'Evening in Paris' or Pond's 'Vanishing Cream', drew up the rear. With heads bowed, eyes cast down and hands joined in saintly fashion, they relished the opportunity to show themselves off in all their finery!

As you clattered down the stairway you had to negotiate your way past the Brilliantine men kneeling on caps and handkerchiefs on either side. Huddled together, they discussed the weather, the latest prices of cattle and farm produce, progress on the farm, how animals had 'wintered' etc. but were not beyond pinching a shapely bottom on its way past. Occasionally, the priest tried to encourage them to fill up the empty seats near the front, but the thought of saying goodbye to their quick get-a-way at the end or 'craic' at the back was too difficult to swallow, and so they gracefully declined his invitation. Apart from the odd immediate shuffle just to keep him happy, things never really changed.

After Mass on Sunday a woman would sometimes appear at the altar rails to be 'churched'.

Canon Michael Kelly P.P.

Father Edward Fox C.C.

This was some form of purification rite – probably based on the old Jewish tradition - deemed necessary or appropriate after childbirth and involved the usual triple treatment of two lighted candles, a set of prayers said by the priest in his surplice and stole and quite a liberal dousing with Holy Water.

Sometimes there was Benediction with Exposition of the Blessed Sacrament after Mass on a Sunday, but generally it took place at six o' clock in the evening. If Latin added a certain mystique to the celebration of the Eucharist, the waft of incense from the swinging thurible, the gold-crusted garb of the priest, his gilded monstrance and invocation of the 'Tower of Ivory', 'House of Gold', 'Arc of the Covenant', 'Mystical Rose' etc. lifted it to a higher plane.

Candles were for ever burning on the heart-shaped brass shrine close to the altar gates. Some with white wicks, paid for in advance, were left unlit awaiting the next action on the altar, others proudly petitioned the Lord on behalf of their donors while a few poor devils, suffering 'burn-out' and in the throes of death, spluttered and splattered their last at the bottom of the grippers.

Once we became proficient in the Latin responses and requisite rubrics, we were ready to serve on the altar. We didn't exactly have shining halos like our sisters but nevertheless we were the ones who got the call!

To St. Mary's we did speed,
And just got there in time to breathe.
Starched surplices and limp suitanes,
Made angelic face and hands!

We brought the water and the wine,
And once enjoyed a 'swig' divine!
We bowed and knelt with sacred graces,
But often tripped on dangling laces.

With nudge and belt we kept others in tow,
But hid from view this Holy Show!
I bet things haven't changed that much,
Still years leave one quite out of touch!

There were certain perks attached to serving on the altar. It provided a good excuse for going late to school and on special occasions, such as baptisms, weddings and funerals, you could 'hit' on the odd good tip. As in every walk in life, there were some plum jobs and some less prestigious positions. Serving on the right was No.1. It meant you led the procession from vestry to altar; you were the one privileged to hit the bell with the special beater and serve the wine to the priest at the Offertory. The fellow on the left was reduced to turning the white cloth across the communion-rails, placing the paten under the chin of communicants and holding up the priest's chasuble at the Consecration. Naturally, all this gave rise to a certain element of competition. The issue was usually settled by seniority but brawn sometimes won out over age!

During the homily and reading of notices, we turned round to face the congregation. We made ourselves as comfortable as possible, leaning on elbows and lounging on the altar steps. Of course, we had to avoid making eye contact with some of our smart friends in the front seats, ever anxious to extract a giggle or two.

Sometimes, we had to escort the priest with lighted candles. I had a certain fascination with the hot wax that flowed, and couldn't resist the temptation to pick at it and mould it into various shapes.

Apart from your ordinary Sunday and the major feasts of Easter and Christmas, there was a whole plethora of holidays of obligation and others earmarked for special devotions: 'The Assumption of Our Lady' (August 15) and 'The Immaculate Conception' (December 8), feast day of St Brigid (February 1), Candlemas Day (February 2), feast day of St. Blaise, patron of throats (February 3), St. Patrick (March 17), St. Joseph (March 25), St. Anthony of Padua (June 13), St. Therese of Lisieux (October 1), Sacred Heart of Jesus (Friday after the 2nd.Sunday after Pentecost), Feast of All Saints (November 1) and the feast of All Souls (November 2). Add in the penitential seasons of Lent and Advent, a rake of First Fridays, First Saturdays and First Sundays, not to speak of a Holy Year in 1950 and a Marian Year in 1954, and there wasn't much room left for secular diversion! 1954 was also the year that Fr. Peyton, a Mayo-born priest of the Congregation of the Holy Cross, known as the 'Rosary Priest', arrived in Ireland with his Family Rosary Crusade. Whatever chance there was that my mother might forget to say the rosary the odd night before then, Fr. Peyton's slogan, 'A family that prays together, stays together', put paid to that!

To cap it all, a few missioners would be called in every four or five years to conduct the 'Parish Mission' so as to rescue the wayward and polish up any tarnished haloes that were knocking about. These were usually Redemptorists – one old 'fire and brimstone' fellow, capable of putting the fear of God in any congregation, and a more restrained 'side kick'. Both were capable of telling the odd good yarn before getting the real proceedings under way. As well as dealing with the semi-saved, they also 'had a go' at calling the odd 'eccentric' to heal. This tiny anti-coercionist lobby sometimes didn't mince their words when telling the holy men where to go or what to do with themselves!

Every evening at eight o'clock for a full week we had to turn up for Rosary, Benediction, Sermon and Confessions. The Sermon was really the main item on the agenda and here the focus was on such topics as Death, Judgement, Damnation and Hell. There was also a smattering on 'company keeping' and sins of the flesh, most of which went over our young heads! Thus, the honest citizens of Swad were formed for eternity. It became crystal clear that any kind of cavorting in lonely places – cuddling behind hay-stacks in Cassidy's meadow, at the back of St. Mary's Hall, down Barney Kellagher's Lane, along the reedy shore of Brackley lake or any 'courting corner' – was simply not on. In actual fact, swimming in the 'Farmer's Hole' was about the only pleasurable activity that went unscathed, and even this demanded discretion with regard to attire.

Resolutions to make a clean start were 'written in stone', armfuls of rosaries, prayer books with ornate gold locks attached to their sides, missals, scapulars, crucifixes and medals, holy pictures of St.Joseph and his lily, Dominic Savio and Maria Goretti, purses with the inscription

'My Rosary' etc. were purchased at the stalls in Chapel Square. Everything seemed most abnormal. It looked as if an epidemic of 'Housemaid's Knee' was 'on the cards'. As luck would have it, the mission had no serious long-term effects! A thaw soon set in and allayed our fears. While our chances of getting past St. Peter seemed quite remote early on, thankfully the odds on this shortened considerably by the time pious objects were being blessed and Satan was being renounced on the closing night! By then we were all quite sad that the missioners were leaving, that the stalls were being taken down and the whole thing was over. We began to appreciate what a great social occasion it really was.

The annual Corpus Christi procession from St. Mary's Church to a special altar, crafted and erected by Terry Greene at the bottom of the village, where Benediction was imparted, was a major communal proclamation of faith.

Houses along the route were specially painted beforehand and garlanded in fresh summer flowers such as roses and lupins. Papal and national flags swayed in the breeze, bunting was linked to dwellings on either side and there were statues, holy pictures and specially prepared mini-altars in windows and doorways along the way.

A cross bearer with escort of acolytes led the procession. The priest carried the Blessed Sacrament in a monstrance beneath a canopy of white and gold, borne by four male parishioners. Girls in First Communion dresses walked backwards, strewing primroses, daisies, bluebells and rose petals from their home-made baskets to create a carpet for the approaching Eucharist while members of the Garda and L.D.F. formed a guard of honour. Children of Mary were dressed in their blue cloaks, banners from different sodalities and confraternities were on display, the choir sang and prayers were recited. People were dressed in their best summer attire and no doubt, welcomed the opportunity to parade fashion. Still, anyone watching alongside would surely have been impressed by the reverence and general devotion.

Finally, priests and people marched back to St. Mary's for further prayers, the final blessing and a very passionate rendering of 'Faith of Our Fathers'.

An army may march on its stomach, but priests at that time needed 'dues' and 'offerings' to survive. I could never really fathom what was the essential difference between the two. You may have owed one as a debt, whereas the other sounded more like a voluntary contribution. Of course some cynic might argue that the word 'voluntary' didn't figure in the ecclesiastical dictionaries of that era!

Funeral 'offerings' were collected at a table near the altar. Here the priest and male relations of the deceased presided and individual contributions, as well as the final tally, were publically acknowledged. Later on, the question, 'How much did he (or she) go for?' was on everyone's lips. The total amount was a well-recognized barometer-type reading of your popularity, albeit after you had gone. Many people wouldn't miss a funeral or neglect to forward their contribution 'for the world' in case they would offend a neighbour. Of course, they also wanted to ensure that when their own time came, they would get a good 'send-off'. This custom of taking up a collection on the occasion of a funeral dated back to the 17th.century and continued until 1974.

Stipends were paid to the priest in return for his saying Mass for a deceased friend or relative or for conducting baptismal and marriage services. He also got tokens for giving letters of freedom to marry outside the parish. You were never left under any illusion but that a very definite sum was required for each service. People put a lot of pressure on themselves by giving Mass cards 'all over the place' and it was not unknown for some to boast about the number they received. The whole thing smacked of buying masses and purchasing your way into Heaven. In fairness to the clergy, an attempt was made to curtail this business but the request fell on deaf ears.

Priests' 'dues'were collected at Christmas, Easter and Pentecost. Prior notice was given as to when the names of subscribers and their contributions would be read out. This was meant to act as a kind of catalyst or incentive to those tempted to waver or delay payment. Needless to say, the system, which remained in vogue until the 1960's, guaranteed the desired response. Each individual earner was levied and the sum paid was a good yardstick of your financial standing in the community. The local doctor and principal teacher usually headed the list and these were closely followed by the wealthiest businessmen in the village.

People were intensely proud of their local parish and diocese. Despite their meager means, they donated generously to the building of the new cathedral of St. Patrick and St. Felim in Cavan (completed in 1942 at a cost of £209,000), to the construction of St. Mary's Hall in the village in 1951 and to the renovation of St. Mary's Church (costing £21,000 - a major sum in 1959).

Of course, there were also Church of Ireland and Methodist communities in our area. The latter was established by Methodist founder and evangelist, John Wesley, who visited the village on several occasions in and around 1769. The Methodists had their church or 'preaching house' (built around 1840) close to the entrance to the Fair Green and their resident preacher lived in the Manse (built in 1890) on the school road.

The members of each community lived in peaceful co-existence and were delighted to help out one another whenever the need arose. Their children went along to their respective schools together and adults ceilidhed over and back. Despite all this, you could still sense that there was a certain divide. No doubt, the Protestants had their own good reasons for keeping us at a safe distance. The Catholic Church's 'Ne temere' decree, issued by Pius X at the turn of the century, didn't help. When a Catholic married a non-Catholic, it required an undertaking from the mixed marriage partners that all children of the marriage be baptized and brought up as Catholics.

The Protestants had their own school run by highly respected teacher, Mrs. Rosina Good (nee Milliken). She came originally from Island Magee, Co. Antrim in 1923, married Mr. John Good and gave dedicated service until she retired in 1962. They also had their own Church services but our knowledge of these was quite sketchy. We knew, for example, that they had their Harvest Thanksgiving Service on a Friday and Sunday evening in October, and that the Scriptures played an important part in their lives, if only from having a squint at the 'Bible Gems' on their kitchen calendars. Hymn singing with great gusto and in parts seemed to be quite central to their rituals.

I don't think their ministers gave the same 'doing' to sins of the flesh as ours. We reckoned they were more into hearing voices from Heaven! This conjecture was based more on idle talk than on any solid evidence.

They had what they called a Select Vestry and some leaders attended a General Synod. We knew that their children went to Sunday school, called the 'Our Father' 'The Lord's Prayer' and that their minister lived in the Rectory beside St.Augustine's Church. The latter, opened on June 19, 1849, and situated on the very edge of the village, can now boast that it is the second oldest building in Swad but back then it seemed to look across rather enviously at its older sibling, St. Mary's (1828), right there at the hub. It probably felt that our place was gloating rather condescendingly at its suburban location! The two churches were built by a local Protestant builder called Nixon. He transported the stones from Gortalugany.

While we never set foot inside the door of St. Augustine's, we did attend the Protestant Sales of Work and bazaars in aid of its re-roofing. Believe it or not, I visited it for the very first time in my life in 2007 when I was invited in by its affable Portadown-born Rector, Rev. Geoff Wilson. He is a man intent on developing a strong community bond. I was in awe at the beautiful stained-glass window depicting the parable of the Prodigal Son and the light that filtered through, not to mention the wonderful sense of peace and quiet that I experienced during my short visit.

Some reckoned 'you would know a Protestant a mile away' because they had a different complexion! One old lady I knew went so far as to attribute their rather pale and yellowish colour to the fact that they did not receive our Holy Communion. Exponents of 'The Protestant Look' thesis were convinced that this colour differential became more pronounced, and therefore, more apparent, coming up to the glorious 'twelfth of July'. Even if you didn't recognize them from their colour, their names gave them away! While the Catholic Mc Governs and Maguires soloed up the field with the right foot, our good Protestant neighbours avoided the off-side trap or kicked for touch with the left!

Many Protestants kept to themselves and had a reputation for going to bed early, getting up 'at the crack of dawn', working hard, living sober lives, being scrupulously honest and the 'best of neighbours. They were also renowned for fair dealing and provided good conditions for their workers. Their fields were neat and indeed their general husbandry often put that of their Catholic neighbours to shame. You got the impression, however vague, that they had a 'soft spot' for England and Northern Ireland, that they got caught on the 'wrong' side of the border and might have been more at home in the Kinawley end of the parish. I don't know exactly how we got that idea. The fact that they read the 'Irish Times' and English periodicals, often listened to the B.B.C. Home Service, went to schools in Northern Ireland and took a great interest in the Royal family may have influenced us in our thinking.

As a child, one thought it odd that Protestant 'priests' got married, had children and lived in a 'Manse' or 'Rectory' rather than in a presbytery or 'Parochial House'. In those pre-Vatican 2 days, we picked up the 'vibes' somewhere along the line that we Catholics had an absolute monopoly or copyright on the truth, that 'we' were right and 'they' were wrong or misguided and we foolishly believed that despite their good living, it would 'take them all their time' to get through the gates of Heaven! With this kind of thinking in vogue, it's hardly surprising that the Vatican Council highlighted our 'need to acquire a more adequate understanding of the respective doctrines of our separated breathren, their history, their spiritual and liturgical life, their religious psychology and general background.' (Unitatis Redintegratio 9 Decree on Ecumenism.)

PRIESTS IN THE PARISH OF KINAWLEY

P.P.'s

Michael Kelly ——— June '44 - September '50 (Transferred)
John J. Murtagh ——— Sept. '50 - August '55 (Died)
Thomas O' Dowd ——— August '55 - March '60 (Died)
Charles J. Matthews ——— May '60 - November '63(Died)

Curates (Kinawley area)

Bernard O' Reilly ——— February '36 – June '43
Laurence Gilmartin ——— June '43 - August '65

Curates (Swanlinbar area)

Patrick O' Reilly ——— February '34 – June '41
Laurence Corr ——— June '41   - March '47
Francis Brennan ——— March '47   - July '54
Edward Fox ——— July '54   - July '74

CHURCH OF IRELAND CLERGY

Rev. Robert Ernest Trenier ——— 1939 - 1944
Rev. Robert John Doonan ——— 1944 - 1950
Rev. John Richard Wheelock ——— 1951 - 1956
Rev. Canon H.I.K. Anderson ——— 1956 - 1957
(In 1957 Templeport parish was amalgamated with Swanlinbar)
Rev. Cecil Armstrong ——— 1957 - 1962

St. Augustine's Church of Ireland built in 1849

Frank Mc Govern, his wife, Maisie, and brother, Dermott, 'winning' the hay at Gortnaleg (Photo. Frank Mc Govern)

THE ANNUAL CYCLE

As most people in the village and surrounding area depended either directly or indirectly on agriculture, their lives were governed by the seasons and revolved around the main seasonal tasks of sowing, reaping and harvesting – not unlike those of the ancient Celts, whose year was also based on the farming cycle. Their special religious rituals at Samhain (November), Imbolg (February), Bealtaine (May) and Lugnasa (August) related to their preoccupations at particular times. Our religion and lives were also intertwined. We witnessed birth, death and resurrection in the new-born chickens, lambs and calves, in the tiny seeds and potato 'cuts' that had to die in order to bring forth an abundance of life-giving food. The gospel parables of the lost sheep, the sower and the seed, the unfruitful fig tree, together with reference to the effect of storm were easily understood by those who earned their daily bread by the sweat of their brows on a family farm.

St. Brigid's day (February 1), the first day of spring, heralded the beginning of the farming year. People made special crosses of rush, placed them in their homes, barns and byres and prayed for the saint's protection and blessing on themselves and their livestock. The weather was usually cold and stormy so apart from spreading farmyard manure or top dressing to promote a higher hay yield, preparing the ground for crops or attending fairs, farmers were mainly engaged in foddering, milking (a regular twice a day routine) and going to the creamery. Some kept a portion of the cream for churning and the production of home-made butter.

Candlemas Day (February 2), the feast of the Purification, which was later linked to the Presentation of the Lord in the temple, was the day when all the candles were blessed. Snowdrops were usually in bloom around this time and so came to be known as 'Candlemas Bells'. Next day we celebrated the feast of St. Blaise, patron of throat illnesses, who was reputed to have saved the life of a boy who got a large fish bone stuck in his throat. There was always a big crowd in St. Mary's when the priest held two candles slightly open and pressed them against our throats. St. Valentine's Day didn't have anything like the profile it has today. We mustn't have been as romantic in those days!

Shrove Tuesday, the eve of the Lenten fast, was a day of self-indulgence, a time 'to stuff your face'! It was a great day for pancakes (a traditional way of using up milk, flour and eggs) and feasting in preparation for the forty days of fasting, abstinence and general self-denial associated with Lent. Young people loved to compete with one another tossing the pancakes high above the flames. The whole scene changed next day, Ash Wednesday.

We'd be out early for Mass and resolve (under some subtle pressure!) to give up sweets for Lent. Adults (21 to 60) had to fast 'unless excused by exhausting labour, infirmity or poverty'. They could only have one full meal and two collations. Everyone over the age of seven had to abstain from eating 'flesh meat and its products' on Wednesdays and Fridays. The priest would thumb a cross on our foreheads, forcibly reminding us that it was from dust we came and unto dust we would return. On Fridays during the holy season, we'd gather in the church for the Stations of the Cross, kneel with the priest as he prayed, 'We adore Thee, O Christ, and praise Thee' and join in the refrain,' Because by Thy holy cross Thou hast redeemed the world'. Trade in Mrs. Reilly's sweet shop, as well as in the local pubs, slumped for a time, but most of the loss was recouped on St.Patrick's day. Then we'd 'tuck into' our cache of goodies, lovingly stored, eyed and carefully tended during the previous weeks. Of course we also had to celebrate the national apostle's gift of faith by lifting the rafters off St. Mary's church with 'Hail Glorious St. Patrick' or 'Dóchas Linn Naomh Pádraig'. He was undoubtedly Britain's greatest gift to Ireland! Later on, the men folk especially would let down their hair, drown the shamrock (when the prohibition on pub opening was lifted) and enjoy Micheál O'Hehir's commentaries on the Railway Cup finals. These were very highly regarded in the '50's with attendance reaching an all-time high of 49,023 in 1954.

There were no dances during Lent so Whist and 25 card drives, bazaars and plays came into their own. The annual parochial bazaar in St. Mary's Hall took precedence over everything else. Parishioners donated most of the prizes, which included items such as tea sets, trays, bread bins, sets of saucepans, holy pictures, jugs and sugar bowls, boxes of chocolates, sweets and biscuits, hot water bottles, alarm clocks, electrical items, bags of potatoes, turf and blocks of timber etc. Lively young girls sold tickets at three pence each or five for a shilling and a spin of the rickety wheel determined the winner. There was also a special door prize and a major draw for a young calf, a half ton of coal, a leg of lamb and a bottle of whiskey on the closing night. The inimitable Tommy Gregory generally acted as M.C. with Master Connaughton and Pat Maguire providing a back-up service. You could also chance your luck at throwing rings, have a shot at the Bull's Eye or join James Curran and Ben Mc Hugh at the Roulette table. Con Darcy, Ben Paddy Johnny and other solid citizens also had key roles in the proceedings, while the women served the best of tea, buns and sandwiches in the 'Mineral Bar'.

The bazaar was an enjoyable social occasion, a wonderful family night out. As well as the raffles and roulette table, there was also a shooting range and a rings competition. Youngsters had a great time sliding through the sawdust that protected the dance floor, and when Fr. Fox's back was turned and the Master wasn't looking, some were more than capable of using the same sawdust for diverse purposes!

Despite all the functions held during Lent, it was still a rather gloomy time of year and we were glad to see the odd primrose and daisy, if only to remind us of brighter days ahead.

Around St.Patrick's day, farmers began to let out their cattle. They had to plough for wheat and other cereal crops, and like the townsfolk, get their potato-planting under way. Arran Banners, Epicures and Kerr's Pinks were popular varieties but my father always liked to sow some early oval-shaped Sharp's Express. He made a special effort to have these in by late February/early March so that they would be ready for eating before the end of June.This meant that he had to devise certain strategies to protect their delicate leaves from the frost when they first peeped out from under the soil.

LENTEN REGULATIONS, 1951

1. (a). All days of Lent (Sundays and 17th March excepted) are days of fast.

   (b). All Wednesdays and Fridays of Lent, are days of fast and abstinence.

2. The law of fasting prescribes that on Fast Days only one principal meal be taken, but permits a collation morning and evening according to recent modifications.

3. All who have completed their twenty-first year and who have not yet entered on their sixtieth year are bound by the law of Fasting, unless excused by exhausting labour, infirmity or poverty.

4. The law of Abstinence forbids the use of flesh meat and its products, such as soup or broth. The products of meat, such as suet, lard or dripping may be used as condiments or for cooking purposes.

5. All over the age of seven years are bound by the law of Abstinence.

6. Parish Priests, for a reasonable cause, and in individual cases, can dispense their parishioners even while these are outside the parish, and outsiders while in the parish, and not only individuals but individual families from the Fast or Abstinence or both. The same privilege is hereby granted to Administrators, and to heads of Colleges in respect of those who live in the College, and to superiors of religious communities of priests, who may dispense their subjects and all others who are attached to, or live in the community. Confessors may dispense their penitents intra tribunal, when none of those previously mentioned can be approached in time to meet the needs of a particular case.

✠ EUGENE O'CALLAGHAN
30th January, 1951.

Lenten Regulations 1951, courtesy of The Fermanagh Herald.

There was always a certain friendly rivalry to see who would have the earliest spuds. People put down a line and went to great rounds generally to ensure that drills and ridges were straight and pleasing to the eye. If a town garden was in the public view, a certain degree of showmanship and competition could be discerned! Pat Woods and Pat Prior had gardens on either side of the New Bridge. Laid out with military precision, they would have captured prizes in any horticultural competition.

The Compulsory Tillage Act passed in 1941 obliged farmers to have a portion of land under crops. By 1944 three-eights of your holding was supposed to be used for this purpose and tillage inspectors came around to ensure that you complied with the directive. It promoted the concept of self-sufficiency and this idea of catering for your family's food needs persisted for many years afterwards.

There was a lot of work involved in potato growing. Apart altogether from planting, the fresh stalks had to be 'shovelled' or 'moulded' and sprayed intermittently with a mixture of copper sulphate (bluestone) and washing soda in order to protect them from the dreaded blight. This operation had to be done before the tiny blue blossoms of the Kerr's Pinks and white blossoms of the Arran Banners appeared and a number of times afterwards depending on the weather. While August was the worst month for blight, people remembered that in 'Black '47' it came in June and so small farmers in particular weren't prepared to take any chances with what was then their priority crop.

The end of February or early March was the lambing season and from then on things began to 'heat up' on the farms. This was also the farmers' last chance to plant vegetables and cereals, animals needed assistance during calving and lambing, and once the corn and potatoes in particular had been taken care of and the weather began to improve, it was time to at least start thinking about going to Tullydermot, Alteen (nowadays pronounced Ilcheen) or Finaghoo to cut back the 'scraith' (top sods) and get the turf cutting under way. 'Tully' (as it was popularly known) in the early 1940's supplied almost two hundred families with their winter fuel supply.

Once the weather began to improve, my mother would order her 'Day Old Chicks' from Mc Cormack's Elmbank hatchery in Cavan. The breeds at that time included Light Sussex, Minorca Black, Rhode Island Red, White Leghorn and White Wyandotte. For some reason or other, she favoured the Rhode Islanders. When these little balls of fluff first arrived, they were housed under the stairs in the pantry, a warm place because it was right behind the chimney breast. There they remained until they were able to withstand cooler conditions. As they grew older, they were given free range- could wander about the yard at will. Despite this, I have a clear memory of their spending a lot of quality time huddled together around our back door. Whenever you opened up, you had to 'Shoo, shoo' them and send them clucking and squawking in all directions. In fairness, they paid their way. The pullets (females) supplied us with eggs while the poor unfortunate cockerels (males) were 'guillotined' and roasted for the Sunday dinner! Of course, some people reared their own chicks from 'scratch' and in the early 50's most took advantage of government grants to build special quarters for the hens. Turkey chicks were also hatched out in the spring time and reared for the Christmas market.

The whole system of egg production changed later on when the 'Deep Litter' method was introduced. Today, you'd look twice if you saw a hen around a house, not to speak of a duck, turkey or goose. Maybe the 'Greens' will bring back the humble hen!

April to early May saw the return of the long-tailed swallow from her winter vacation in South Africa. She proceeded to build her saucer- shaped mud nest in some new outhouse or else opted for her former site. The short fork-tailed house martins, smaller but somewhat similar in appearance, got theirs organized around the same time under the eaves of houses. Two other wonderful migratory heralds of Spring also arrived; the elusive corncrake with her repetitive grating 'creck-creck' or was it 'aic-aic' that seemed to go on all night and the courting cuckoo with his equally repetitive 'cuck-oo'. We were all 'au fait' with the latter's movements from learning the following by heart-

'In April, come he will,
In May, he sings all day,
In June, he changes her tune,
In July, he makes ready to fly
And in August go he must

As soon as the soil warmed up and the gardener turned his first sod, the plump, short-necked, cheeky little robin with her distinctive orange-red face and breast, who remained with us over the winter months, was sure to put in an appearance. With her pronounced 'tik-tik' she was just as anxious to establish her territory and attract mates as she was to snap up a nice juicy worm!

April 6 was the beginning of the tax year, but that didn't bother too many of the citizens of Swad. Some traders may have had plenty of 'oul' shillings' stored away under the mattress from their smuggling days during the war, and didn't have to worry unduly about the four month Irish bank dispute that began in December 1954. Like some of their northern neighbours, it was a question of 'what we have we hold'!

On Palm Sunday the priest blessed the yew branches and we held these aloft, reminiscent of the fickle multitude, who greeted Jesus' triumphal entry into Jerusalem. We took the blessed palm home and placed it behind some holy picture. On Holy Thursday we had the re-enactment of the Last Supper and the washing of the feet. Afterwards, the Blessed Sacrament was removed from the tabernacle and taken to the 'Altar of Repose'. The door was left open until Easter Sunday. During the intervening period all crucifixes and statues were draped in purple. Good Friday was a day of fast and abstinence when the main ceremony included a long detailed account of the Lord's Passion and the 'veneration' of the Cross. On Easter Sunday, we celebrated the Resurrection of the Lord. We got up early to see the sun dancing in joy and competed to see who would eat the most eggs! If the weather was fine, the competition would continue out in the back garden. Staunch Republicans sported their Easter lilies around this time.

The month of May was dedicated to the Virgin Mary and small altars in her honour were erected in homes and schools. 'Bring Flowers of the Rarest' was the 'in' hymn at this time.

Children scattered primroses on the doorsteps – an ancient custom to keep away evil spirits. May Day or Bealtaine, as it was known in Celtic times, was associated with growth and fertility.'Twas then that great bonfires were lit in honour of the sun, people danced and made merry and 'The Little People' moved from their winter to summer residences. For us too it announced the coming of summer and of course, it was the start of the G.A.A. championships. It could be quite cold at night with the odd touch of frost. So you'd hear people say, 'Don't cast a clout 'til May be out'.

May was also the month for the bog. Large government advertisements in the papers on May 1 1943 encouraged people to cut twice as much as in 1942 and to get down to it right away. Turf was a vital form of fuel, especially during the war, when coal was unobtainable. Banks were stripped of their scraith (top sods), the turf was cut with a slean and spread. After a week or so, depending on the weather, it was 'footed', later 'clamped' and finally wheeled or carried by ass and creels to be stacked near the roadway. Children, especially, loved the feel of the squelchy wet peat on the bare feet and an egg boiled in a black saucepan in the bog was hard to beat. Midges there could drive you insane but 'freewheeling' home afterwards with the cool breeze in your face was surely one of life's greatest pleasures. The merry month of May was the time when cattle were let out to pasture and sheep onto the hills but there was also lots of weeding to be done. Rain during this month promoted grass growth but hindered work in the bog. So, not everyone would have agreed with the traditional rhyme:

'A wet May and a dry June
Make the farmer whistle a tune'.

Beautiful flowers bloomed around this time- wallflowers, lupins, marigolds, the lilac with its distinctive smell, sweet pea, and of course the rose came into its own in June. Gladioli, dahlias, chrysanthemums and Sweet William were also popular.

If everything went according to plan, the turf would be drawn home in June before haymaking began but very often this task had to be put on the long finger until September. June, the month dedicated to the Sacred Heart, was also the month in which several locals opted to 'do' Lough Derg, a three day penitential pilgrimage that ran from June 1 until August 15. Bonfires were lit on the evening of June 23 (St. John's Eve) - a custom dating back to Celtic times. After June 29 or early in July, whenever the weather was fine, Joe Leonard, Mickey P, Andy, Phil Mac and others would be out 'on the country' all day and sometimes well into the night, cutting meadow. Sheep were sheered and dipped around this time.

July 1 was the beginning of the national school year. New teacher appointees took up their positions and 'scholars' changed classes. Those starting off had two weeks to settle in before the summer holidays commenced. The children got an extended break in 1946. An I.N.T.O. teachers' strike left 40,000 without class from March 20 until October 31.

The month was often referred to as 'Hungry July' because most of the main crops- apart from some early potatoes, such as Epicures, British Queens and May Queens, that were dug around the 12th. - were not ready as yet. On the last Sunday in the month, a few hardy local

Petticoat power to the fore in Gortnaleg as Ita, Anne and Eileen Mc
Govern keep a tight grip on the reins! (Photo: Frank Mc Govern)

Jimmy Whelan and John Devine bringing home the bacon Swad style! (Photo: Elsie (Howden) Abbott)

climbers headed to Mayo to scale Croagh Patrick. 100, 000 from all over Ireland climbed 'The Reek' in 1950.

August 15 was a great day for Annual Sports. These were held regularly in places like Ballyconnell, Belcoo and Derrylin and young people especially cycled long distances to attend or compete. Sports were also held in Mac's field but on a less regular basis.

Haymaking was a mammoth task and usually ran well into August or even early September in a bad year. In 1946, which was one of the wettest years on record, the All-Ireland final became known as 'Save the Harvest final' because it had to be postponed until October to give people a chance to save the hay. In 1958 we had one of the wettest autumns and winters in living memory and this caused terrible devastation on the farms. On the other hand, there was a long, hot summer in 1959 when saving the harvest proved to be no bother at all. Once the hay was removed from the meadows, cattle were delighted to leave the bare fields and savour the lush green 'after-grass'.

September was the main month for harvesting grain crops. In the early days, the corn was cut with a scythe. A good man could lay an acre in a day. Later, horse mowers were used. The stalks were gathered, tied into sheaves, made into stooks and stacked. They were left in the field for some time before being taken to the haggard and made into larger stacks. The threshing took place later in the year. The work of the horse mower was replaced by the reaper and binder. Finally the combine harvester did all the work.

As children we loved to go out picking blackberries and apples in September. P. Kavanagh from Crumlin in Dublin bought some of these blackberries and apples, as well as damsons and vegetable marrow, from local agents.

The last of the turf had to be brought home. Spuds were also dug and pitted in September and October. Kerr's Pinks were at their very best in September but the main crop wasn't harvested until October. Some young people were delighted to help out with the picking. Like making laps, it was a backbreaking job but it provided a legitimate excuse for taking a few days off school! Pitting involved making a mound of the crop on a bed of straw or dried rushes, covering it with more of the same and finally topping it off with clay. Turnips, that earlier on had been laboriously weeded and thinned, were pulled.

The All-Ireland hurling and football finals were played in September. So, it was the high point in the G.A.A. calendar. It was also the month when swallows, swifts and martins prepared to depart and head to warmer climes.

Halloween (October 31) was once marked by the Celtic festival of Samhain, the Lord of Death. It was supposed to be a ghost or spirit night. There was an old tradition that the souls of the dead returned to their family homes that night. In our day, it was a merrymaking time for young and old. If there was such a thing as a season of plenty, this was it. There was boxty, bacon, barm brack and lots of fruit and vegetables. We used to go out to Cullen's Rock to collect the hazel nuts. As soon as darkness set in, we let off blasts from our carbide tin 'bombs'. There was great excitement in the kitchen that night as we competed to extract sixpence from a basin quarter full of water with mouth only, or bite the apple hanging from the roof without using our hands. Whoever got the ring from the barmbrack was destined to be first up the aisle!

November was the month of the 'Suffering Souls in Purgatory'. Around the feast of St. Martin (November 11) as in springtime, when the weather was nice and cool, the fattened pig was killed to ensure that there would be a good supply of bacon, many a family's main source of protein. One rope was tied to his front leg, another to the one at the back on the opposite side. Two men pulled these in opposite directions and thus the poor fellow was grounded. He generally got a few belts on the head with a mallet, was stabbed through the heart and was then hung up for some time before being doused with hot water and shaved. After that he was cut up on the kitchen table, the meat was salted, put in a tea-chest and stored in the coldest place in the house.

November was also the time when fields were ploughed and the cattle were brought in from the pastures. Apart from his having to fodder and milk his cattle, November, December and indeed January were not particularly busy months for the farmer, so he got a chance to look after his ditches and drains and repair any farm equipment that needed attention. He also had time to buy his copy of Old Moore's Almanac with all its predictions and have them well and truly digested before the new season began. His wife got her 'American Bronze' turkeys and/or geese ready for the Christmas market. They fetched about 2/6 a pound and this 'pin money' often served to pay off outstanding household bills.

Christmas was special – a kind of coral island in time with its plum pudding wrapped in gauze, Brian O' Higgins cards with their Gaelic motifs and others depicting sleighs and reindeers, all ranged across the piano and mantlepiece. Every picture and sill had a sprig of holly, well adorned with red berries and the turkey hung full length from the rafters in the turf-shed. Paper-decorations and the few clusters of balloons dangling from the ceiling in the sitting room gave the place a real 'lift'. There was the usual panic when the fairy lights on the Christmas tree refused to work or when the crib's donkey or angel went missing, but everything seemed to come together on the day.

Throughout this season everyone seemed to be 'on top of the world' and in a generous mood. The red glow from the Sacred Heart lamp on the mantel shelf seemed warmer and brighter than ever. Fairy lights blinked and if there was even a skiff of snow, you'd think you were in Switzerland.

We looked forward to the season for weeks. There was great emphasis on the Baby Jesus and Santa Claus. I helped my father axe the huge blocks of wood into smaller units for the sitting room fire and wrote to Santa. Inside, my mother and sisters were busy with the plum puddings, mince-pies and Christmas cake.

On Christmas Eve, we listened intently to the wireless to hear Santa calling out the names from his list of Irish children. Once news filtered through that he had set off from the North Pole, we left a glass of port and some cake by the fireplace in the sitting-room, hung up our stockings, rushed off to bed and pulled the blankets well over our heads. My older sister might peep out from behind the curtain and announce that she could see his light down Felix's lane, but we were too scared to check her out. Instead, we opted to count sheep and nod off.

Next morning, there was bedlam as we screeched with excitement, marvelling at the hair from Santa's beard on the empty glass and the left-over crumbs from his slice of Christmas cake. We tore open our presents and then rushed up to show our parents what we got. Even though my father was probably 'dog tired' and 'at the end of his tether', having worked very late the night before, he still made a special effort to share our wonder at Santa's generosity.

When we grew older, we sometimes cycled to midnight Mass in Kinawley where the church was always ablaze with candle light. You could sense the warmth of the small, intimate community there and the close bond between priest and people. We rode home, muffled to the chin, 'crunching the wafer ice on the pot-holes' (Kavanagh). Stars twinkled, candles flickered in the windows to signify a welcome for St. Joseph and the Blessed Virgin and dogs barked anxiously as we passed by. Sometimes a star would fall from the sky and we knew that another soul was on its way to Heaven. There was no midnight mass in Swad. It had been discontinued before our time because of the risk of disturbance from drunks staggering out of the pubs. Seemingly, they were drawn, as if by magnet, to the music and the light!

On Christmas morning we all gathered around the crib and paid our respects to baby Jesus. There was no place open on Christmas day. It was seen as a family day and everyone stayed at home. As Canon Sheehan in 'Glenanaar' said, it was a matter of honour for Irish families to 'have their fireside consecrated against all intrusion on that day'. Dinner was special, not just because of the goose, turkey, duck, pig's ham, plum pudding or whatever else was on offer, but because it was symbolic of the family bond. Anyone who could possibly turn up, irrespective of distance by land, sea or air or weather conditions, made it to the table while family members, who had died or couldn't come home, were fondly remembered. It was a time to reminisce, a time when many a quiet tear was shed. It was also a time when everyone hoped to be alive and well the following Christmas, a wish beautifully captured in the old Irish prayer,

'Go mbeirimid beo ar an am seo arís'.

On St.Stephen's day, the Wren Boys (or Mummers), dressed in disguise and conical straw hats, would call around to the houses, sometimes carrying or supposedly carrying a wren in a small gaudy box. They would dance, sing, play music and call out,

'The wren, the wren, the king of the birds,
On St. Stephen's Day was caught in the furze;,
Up with the kettle and down with the pan,
 Pray give us a penny to bury the wran.'
Later on they would spend 'the takings' and enjoy their 'Wren Party'.

'Little Christmas' or Nollaig na mBan on January 6 marked the end of the Christmas season. Traditionally, men did all the work that day but if my memory serves me correctly, this didn't happen too often in the Swad of the 50's!

The annual Fianna Fail bazaar, which was held in Woods's Town Hall, always began on the third night of Christmas. It was run by Frank Reilly (M.C.), John O' Brien, Master James Curran, Hubie Dolan and Paddy Mc Hugh from Gubnafarna. Initially, this closely knit group operated under the guidance of James Charles (J.C.) Brady and Sean Lee from Belturbet but once weaned, they took off on their own! They enjoyed the occasional break for refreshments behind the stage until November 1954 when a huge flood in the Claddagh took their 'canteen' all the way to Lough Erne! Undeterred, the 'Soldiers of Destiny' still managed to keep the show on the road and send the punters home with buckets of cheer!

Apart from the Christmas period, December was pretty drab. It was the darkest month and the one with the longest nights. We looked forward to seeing the jackdaw make a shape at building his nest and usher in a new cycle.

The Red Sunbeam Showband: (l.to r.) Sean Gilheany *(Tenor Sax)*, John Murphy, Dublin *(Guitar)*,
Larry Roche, Cork *(Clarinet/Sax)*, Angela Canning, Ballinamore *(Piano)*, Johnny Burgoin, Belfast *(Vocals)*,
Joe Gilheany *(Double Bass)*, Ben Curran, Ballinamore *(Trumpet)*, Joey Gilheany *(Trombone)*,
and James 'Jazzy' Mc Govern (Kinawley) *(Drums)*

POPULAR MUSIC AND DANCING

Every generation can look back and recall favourite songs. Those who lived during World War 2 will no doubt think of Vera Lynn's 'We'll Meet Again' and 'The White Cliffs of Dover', Bing Crosby's 'White Christmas'(played on the wireless for the first time on Christmas day 1941), Gracie Field's 'Run Rabbit Run', Flanagan and Allen's 'We're Gonna Hang Out the Washing on the Siegfried Line' and perhaps the later hits such as Issy Bonn's 'Let Bygones be Bygones (1946), 'Hear My Song, Violetta' (1947) or 'I'm Looking Over a Four Leaf Clover'(1948).

My interest in music really began around the time the first U.K. 'Top Ten', published by the New Musical Express, was introduced in November '52. I associate the song, 'I Saw Mamma Kissing Santa Claus' with that era. 1952 was also a significant year for Irish music. It was then that the newly formed Comhaltas Ceoltoiri Eireann, which was established to foster Irish music, held its first All-Ireland Fleadh Cheoil in Monaghan. These feiseanna would go from strength to strength during the '50's just like the ceilidh bands that reached the pinnacle of their popularity during that same decade. The latter benefited greatly from the advent of the radio and programmes such as Sean Ó' Murchú's famous 'Ceilidhe House'. I have wonderful memories of listening to Brian Lawler's Ardellis, the Kilfenora, Euguene Leddy's and the Aughrim Slopes ceilidhe bands before heading off to bed on a Saturday night.

Irish music also benefited from the establishment of Gael-Linn, from Sean Ó' Riada's research and programme, 'Our Irish Heritage', as well as from Walton's music programme on Radio Eireann. This was presented by Leo Maguire. Every Saturday it advertised the company's song publications, sheet music and new Glenside recordings. Ciarán Mac Mathúna, well known broadcaster and music collector also worked wonders for Irish traditional music. He recorded it around the country and presented it on radio programmes such as 'Ceol Tire', 'A Job of Journeywork', 'Humours of Donnybrook' and later in 1970, 'Mo Cheol Thu'. During his visit to America in 1962, he heard the Clancy Brothers and Tommy Makem and was so impressed he played them on his radio shows. Two years later, one third of all albums sold in Ireland were the Clancys. From the time they appeared on the Ed Sullivan Show, they had already started to popularize Irish music in the U.S.A.

In 1953 the 'Top Ten' became compulsive listening for most young people. They tuned in to Radio Luxembourg. Novelty songs and ballads e.g. the quasi-religious one, 'I Believe', inspired by the Korean War and sung by Frankie Laine, did well. So too did Diana Decker's 'Poppa Piccolino', Guy Mitchell's 'Look At That Girl' and 'She Wears Red Ribbons'. Perry Como's 'Don't Let the Stars Get in Your Eyes' was also popular. Country and Western fans – and there were many of these in rural Ireland- enjoyed Jim Reeve's new release, 'Bimbo'.

In 1954, we had Eddie Calvert's 'Oh Mein Papa', Dorris Day's 'Secret Love', David Whitfield's 'Cara Mia', Little Richard's 'Tuti Fruti' and a host of others. Ruby Murray's 'Heartbeat' made the U.K. Top 5. Sam Phillips, owner of Memphis's Sun Records, who reckoned that if he ' could find a white man with the Negro sound and the Negro feel' he would 'make a billion dollars', had his prayers answered when Elvis Presley walked in the door and ensured that 'Rock 'n Roll' would take off.

In 1955, Lonnie Donegan, the 'King of Skiffle', gave us the memorable 'Rock Island Line' while the popular Belfast-born Ruby Murray had five singles simultaneously in the British Top 20. Her 'Softly, softly' came in at No 1. Eddie Calvert's 'Cherry Pink and Apple Blossom White', Slim Whitman's 'Rose Marie', Jimmy Young's 'The Man from Laramie' and of course, Tennessee Ford's 'We're Gonna Rock Around The Clock' also spent some time at the top.

'Rock 'n Roll' music began to take over in '56 with Chuck Berry's 'Roll Over Beethoven', Fats Domino's 'Blueberry Hill', Carl Perkin's 'Blue Suede Shoes', Elvis Presley's 'Hound Dog' and Gene Vincent's 'Be Bopa Lula' all doing well. We also had Ronnie Hilton's 'No Other Love', Dean Martin's 'Memories Are Made of This', Dorris Day's 'Whatever Will Be Will Be' and Johnny Ray's 'Just Walkin the Rain'. Bridie Gallagher (from Cresslough in Donegal but living in Belfast) released her first single record, 'A Mother's Love's A Blessing'. This would lead to her first L.P – 'The Girl from Donegal' which was to include her most famous recording, 'The Boys from The County Armagh'.

In '57, it was nearly all 'Rock 'n Roll' – 'That'll Be the Day' by the Crickets (with Buddy Holly), Elvis's 'All Shook Up' and 'Jailhouse Rock' and Lee Lewis's 'Great Balls Of Fire'. 'See you later alligator' and the reply, 'in a while, crocodile' from Bill Haley's song became the 'in' parting words! Bill and his rock group, 'The Comets' got a tumultuous reception when they arrived in London. Harry Belafonte's 'Mary's Boy Child' was also a very popular No. 1. In 1957 Patsy Clyne, the great Country singer, got her break on television with 'Walking after Midnight'.

1958 was the year Elvis's 'Jailhouse Rock' topped both the U.S. and U.K. charts. It was also the year that his 'Hound Dog' became only the third record to exceed three million copies sold in the U.S.(Bing Crosby's White Christmas' and Gene Autrey's 'Rudolf The Red Nosed Reindeer' were the other two). Conway Twitty's 'It's Only Make Believe' as well as Perry Como's 'Magic Moments', the Elvery Brothers 'All I Have To Do Is Dream' and Connie Francis's 'Carolina Moon' all reached No 1. Nearer home, the Royal Showband had their first date outside of their native Waterford when on St. Patrick's night they played in the Olympia ballroom in Dublin.

In '59, Russ Conway, the pianist, had two wonderful hits, 'Side Saddle' and 'Roulette'. Other great successes were Shirley Bassey's 'As I Love You', Elvis's 'A Fool Such As I', Bobby Darin's 'Dream Love' and Craig Douglas's 'Only 16' and 'What Do You Want To Make Those Eyes At Me For'. At the end of July that year, Cliff Richards had his first No 1 hit with 'Living Doll'. There were at least three other very significant events, certainly from an Irish perspective. Claddagh records was established, the Clancy brothers and Tommy Makem came together to form what was destined to be a very popular music group and on Easter Sunday the Royal Showband went full-time. Soon afterwards (in 1962) they would record 'Katie Daly' and some time later, 'Kiss Me Quick', the first No 1 single in the Irish charts by a showband.

ST. MARY'S HALL, SWANLINBAR
OPENING NIGHT

SUNDAY, 18th MARCH, 1951
GRAND

VARIETY CONCERT

Doors open 7.30 : Curtain 8 p.m.
TICKETS: 3/- (reserved) & 2/6

St. Mary's Hall. It was built on the site of Byrne's old forge. Inset advert for Variety concert, courtesy Fermangh Herald.

The former 'Wonderland Ballroom', Bawnboy, Co. Cavan. In the late 50's and 60's, it was something of a 'Mecca'
for dancers from West Cavan, South Fermanagh, South Leitrim, and much further afield.

Many of us, who grew up in or near Swad in the '50's, got our first taste of dancing at Andrew 'Big Hugh' Mc Govern's open air Crossroads sessions at Dernacrieve (which were beginning to die out around this time), at the 'Record Hops', organized by a few of the girls, or at the Sinn Fein ceilidhes in Woods's Town Hall. Slightly older and more adventurous 'lemons' may also recall their first forays into the exotic surrounds of Drumbrick, Derrada, the Workhouse in Bawn, Glan Hall or even the galvanized cathedral that was Tonlegee! From these one progressed to the 'Grand' dances in St. Mary's new hall at the bottom of the town. Here, after much hesitation and great trepidation, we rose from our forms on the left, crossed the floor and asked one of the bee-hived brood on the right out for a quickstep, slow foxtrot or waltz, or in reality to step on one another's toes! With a bit of luck this hazardous trek and that immortal ice-breaking query, 'Do you come here often?' could lead to the 'Mineral Bar', crucial last dance and chance to 'walk her home'. Of course there was often some fellow home from England with drainpipe trousers, wedge-soled suede shoes and 'the Tony Curtis look' ready to wipe your eye before you got off the ground.

With the advent of the 'Showband Era' our winkle-pickered feet itched for the new 'breeze block basilicas'. We squeezed into Tommie Reilly's and Oliver Jones's taxis and 'in a pinch' settled for such places as the Star Ballroom, Ballyconnell (that opened to the strains of Ralph

Sean Gallagher (Bundoran), lead singer with the Carnegie Showband.

Sylvester and his orchestra on February 11, 1949), the Wonderland, Bawnboy, St. Ninnidhe's Hall, Derrylin and John Mc Givern's 'Rainbow Ballroom of Romance', Glenfarne with its dimmed lights and 'Romantic Interlude'. On occasions, we even risked eternal damnation by jiving or 'Twisting' like Chubby Checker outside the diocese at 'Fenaghville' with its 2 a.m. closing time!

Most of the bands in the early 50's still had an orchestral approach. Musicians tended to sit behind their music stands and present their repertoire of Irish folk and ceilidhe music, as well as some 'hits' of the day. Those who couldn't read the 'stuff' turned the pages from time to time just to give the impression that they could! All included a mix of slow and fast numbers and of course there was the inevitable 'Ladies' Choice'.

Bands that played in Swad around this time included the Derrylin Starlight Dance band, Dave Dixon's and Pat Mc Mahon's from Clones, Kevin Woods, the Savoy, Jimmy Sturrock from Strabane, Jimmy Shiels from Dundalk, Jack Ruane, Maurice Lynch, Golden Eagle and a host of others. But one of the most popular of them all was our very own 'Red Sunbeam' led by Sean Gilheany from Dernacrieve. Sean's mother was a gifted concertina player while his father 'could make the fiddle talk.' The saxophone was Sean's own favourite and he started off with Tim Fitz's famous band from Milltown. In March 1951, he assembled his own orchestra with brother Joe on the fiddle, James 'Jazzy' Mc Govern on the drums, Robbie Wilson on the piano accordion, Maureen 'Bartley' Mc Govern on piano and Frankie Johnson as vocalist. They 'went down a treat' at the annual Kinawley Emmets Band Ball in the Town Hall in Swad and everyone predicted they would go places. They did – touring all over Ireland as well as performing in dance halls across Britain during the Lenten season each year. Other musicians joined Sean at different times over the years- Joey (Joe's son) played the trombone before linking up with Joe Dolan and the 'Drifters', Ben Curran, a trumpet player, Aidan Canning, another trombone player later to become one of the 'Savoy Swing Seven', Angela Canning and Sean Gallagher, a wonderful vocalist from Bundoran (destined to lead his own band, 'The Quarrymen') to name but a few.

Sean's band adapted to change, embraced the challenges of the 'Showband Era' and eventually teed up with John and Valerie Mc Manus from Derrylin to form the 'Carnegie Showband'. To day Sean and his wife, Josie, are enjoying a quieter life style in idyllic surroundings. Several of their grandchildren are promising musicians and will no doubt carry on the very proud family tradition.

In the mid to late '50's, some notable changes were beginning to surface. Bands from overseas, such as Bill Haley and his Comets, shook off the more sedate approach associated with many of the older 'sit-down' bands. They were 'all go' on stage with lead singers gyrating to their ecstatic fans. Soon Irish bands, clad in colourful blazers or snazzy suits, began to imitate their antics. Lead singers, such as Brendan Bower, Joe Dolan, Dickie Rock, Joe Mac and Brendan O' Brien, were now out in front establishing rapport with their audiences and getting them going. Band numbers were reduced and special celebrity acts were introduced. The old piano, a sacred instrument for generations, had to make way for the new but more 'plasticy' electric organ. While most of the other instruments were retained, it was the guitar that became the whole rage. Thus we witnessed a new and exciting musical phenomenon that would reach its height during the next decade.

Mullan Bridge. This bridge, situated at Mullan, one mile from Swanlinbar on the main Swanlinbar-Enniskillen road, was blown up by the I.R.A. in 1961 during the final phase of the 'Operation Harvest' campaign.

(Photo: Kelvin Boyes Photography)

Operation Harvest and Aftermath

The Cavan/Fermanagh border region close to Swanlinbar remained quiet during 'The Emergency' (1939-1945), apart from the odd exciting confrontation between smugglers and Customs men. The Local Defence Force (L.D.F.), under the watchful eye of its officer, Joseph Connaughton and drill sergeant, Mick Mc Caffrey, carried out its nightly patrols, and proudly brandishing their American 'Springfield' rifles, ensured that people's worst fears of a German or British incursion were never realized! A group of Canadian soldiers, possibly with a few jars on board, did enter Swad on one occasion. This sent alarm bells ringing but our army rose magnificently to the challenge and soon 'silence surged softly back'.

All this was to change when the I.R.A., under the guidance of Sean Cronin, a former army officer turned journalist, launched its military campaign, codenamed 'Operation Harvest', on 12th December 1956. The I.R.A. leaders (including Tony Magan, Tomás Mac Curtain and Paddy Mc Logan) had decided not to include Belfast in the campaign. They were afraid that the organization there had been infiltrated by a mole or two and that it might not be able to defend nationalist areas in the event of a Protestant backlash. They did not want any inter-communal bloodshed. They opted to focus instead on certain border areas. Nationalist South Fermanagh, where two I.R.A. flying columns (codenamed 'Pearse' and 'Teeling') were stationed, was one of those targeted for assault. It was also chosen as the entry point for arms into the north, certainly for the first salvo. It was no surprise then that Swad and its surrounds became something of a war zone. Extra gardai were drafted in, check-points were put in place and the army was conspicuous by its presence. From time to time explosions and gun fire could be heard as Mullan hut was blown to smithereens, barracks in nearby Kinawley and Derrylin were attacked (the latter on several occasions) and the I.R.A. exchanged fire with the British army. Some people were subjected to inquisitions regarding their movements and sightings but they afforded the traditional minimum response – a monotonous series of 'no's' or a stony 'no comment'! People were often searched and suspects were arrested and sometimes even jailed. By December 1957 167 in all were interned.

No sooner had the campaign started than bridges and unapproved roads straddling the border were blown up or spiked by the British army. This may have made life difficult for the guerilla fighters returning south, but it certainly caused terrible hardship, especially to farmers and travellers, and trade in local pubs and other businesses hit an all-time low. The influx of gardai, who could earn substantial overtime, did, however, bring in some extra cash and kept the landladies on their toes. It also brought a welcome batch of eligible suitors for local girls. Many a romance blossomed next to a check-point 'neath the hungry hills of Cuilcagh at that time!

A myriad of factors contributed to the initiation of this 'Border campaign': Republicans' frustration with the verbal gesturing but inactivity of Southern politicians with regard to partition, the release of Republican prisoners after the war, the work of the Anti-Partition League, the gerrymandering of constituencies and discrimination in housing and employment against Catholics in Northern Ireland. However, none of these factors might have roused the I.R.A. from its mid-1940's one-eyed slumber and given it a new lease of life if it hadn't been for the British government's reaction to John Costello's declaration of a 26 county Republic in 1949. It's Ireland Act, passed in the House of Commons on 3rd. May 1949, which attempted to copperfasten the existing partition of Ireland, met with stern opposition in the South. The slogan, 'Border must go', began to appear all over the place.

Events in other parts of the world may also have had an impact on thinking at the time. The ideas of freedom, independence and equality were very much in the air. In 1956, for example, the Hungarians rose up against their Russian invaders, Pakistan declared itself a republic, Tunisia, Morocco and Sudan became independent, General Nasser of Egypt nationalized the Suez canal and Britain (now playing second fiddle to the U.S.A.) had to climb down after U.N./U.S. intervention, Yasser Arafat co-founded the AL FATAH (the PNL) movement. Following Rossa Park's action, the Supreme Court in the U.S.A. ruled that segregation on transportation was unconstitutional while third-class carriages on British rail were abolished. The success of Sinn Fein candidates, Tom Mitchell (Mid-Ulster) and Phil Clarke (Fermanagh/South Tyrone) who obtained 152,310 votes in the 1955 Westminster elections indicated to the I.R.A. leadership that they would have substantial support on the ground.

Some members of the I.R.A. had been focusing on an armed attack from the time they reorganized in the late 40's. In 1951 they established a Military Council to acquire arms and organize a fight for the North. They proceeded to carry out bloodless raids on various police and army establishments – Ebrington barracks in Derry (June 1951) - where raiders 'made off' with 12 rifles, 20 Sten guns and 8 machine guns, Felsted, Essex (July 1953), and a very daring raid on Gough barracks in Armagh in June 1954 in which they seized 250 Lee Enfield rifles, 37 sub machine guns, 9 Bren guns and 40 training rifles without firing a single shot. The latter had been masterminded by Eamon Boyce, the Dublin intelligence officer, with the help of Sean Garland, who infiltrated the barracks in advance. Another raid on Omagh barracks in November 1954 was unsuccessful.

The earliest incidents in what came to be known as the 'Border Campaign' were not part of 'Operation Harvest'. They were carried out by Liam Kelly's Fianna (Saor) Uladh in 1955 and 1956. In actual fact the I.R.A. operation, which was due to start on November 11, '56, was delayed until December 12 because of Saor Uladh's activities.

The I.R.A. plan was to drive out the Crown forces and establish 'an independent, united, democratic Irish Republic' - a rather ambitious (or should I say naive) project for a small group, mainly from the South, with minimal training and limited knowledge of northern territory. The British army was to be its prime target with no question of attacking civilians or policemen, North or South

Initially, it was decided to launch a campaign of civil disobedience and non co-operation and then follow on with a full-blooded, intensive military assault. This plan was abandoned for different reasons. The younger and more impatient members of the organization felt that having accumulated a fairly large armament, they should use force right away. They had their way but most commentators today agree that the campaign would have had a much greater impact if the original strategy had been adopted.

During the opening months, the I.R.A. focused on a series of spectacular raids on police barracks. They also targeted bridges, border posts and other government buildings. The most daring assault was that carried out by the Pearse Column from Lisnaskea on Brookeborough R.U.C. station on the evening of January 1st.1957. This ill-fated attack was led by Sean Garland, assisted by men from Dublin (5), Galway (2), Fermanagh (2), Limerick (1), Monaghan (1), Armagh (1), Wexford (1) and Cork (1). Here 27 year old Sean South from Henry Street in Limerick, who was in charge of the covering group, was killed by a hail of bullets. His Monaghan comrade, 19 year old Fergal O' Hanlon, was badly injured and died a short time later in a cow byre at Baxter's Cross. They became the new Republican martyrs.

The heroism of the small band of I.R.A. men, dedicated to their cause, who fought against impossible odds – close to 3,000 full-time R.U.C. men, a large contingent of trigger-happy 'B-Specials' (Ulster Special Constabulary) and the backing of the British army-stirred and fired our youthful minds at a very impressionable age. Some wrote them off as 'hopeless visionaries' but we were gobsmacked by the fact that 'they weighed so lightly what they gave' – just like the men in Yeats's 'Easter 1916'.

Sean South. and Fergal O Hanlon.

Some 'Operation Harvest' incidents in our area

30/12/56   23 year old Constable John Scally was killed during a second attack on Derrylin police station in the space of three weeks.

31/12/56   Seven men arrested outside Ballyconnell. They were transported to Dublin and charged under the Offences against the State Act.

8/1/57   Sean Cronin arrested in Belturbet and sentenced to three months in prison. Document with plans for guerilla warfare trainingg on Cuilcagh mountain found in his home. John Joe Mc Girl also sentenced at Ballinamore Court around this time.

7/3/57   Cecil Henderson, a mobilized B-Special, was wounded during what was the third attack on Derrylin police station.

10/8/57   Mullen hut badly damaged.

2/12/57   Police vehicle with four men on board ran over a landmine near Cassidy's Cross but no one was injured.

30/12/57   A B-Special's hall at Derrylin was blown up.

15/7/58   29 year old Volunteer Patrick Mc Manus, full-time I.R.A. organizer and O/C of the South Fermanagh Active Service Unit from Kinawley, was killed as he attempted to remove a bomb from a ditch at Derryrealt near Swanlinbar. His two companions, John Owens and Peter Mc Govern, were injured and taken to Cavan Surgical hospital.

24/8/58   26 year old James Crossan from Aughavas, Co. Leitrim but living in Cloneary, Bawnboy since 1950, was shot dead by the R.U.C. near Mullan hut. His companion, 23 year old Ben Mc Hugh, was arrested, taken to Kinawley police station and later transferred to Crumlin Road jail, where he was interned until his release on 30th. April 1961. Both men were unarmed. Later, John Tully of Clann na Poblachta tried unsuccessfull to organize a full enquiry into James Crossan's death.

8/9/58   Orange Hall in Kinawley, used by B-Specials for training, was blown up. Windows shattered in St. Naile's Church and in local Primary school.

11/1/60   Garda came across three armed men in British army uniforms in a hayshed near the village. They fled, leaving behind a quantity of guns and ammunition.

12/8/60   Garda made a further haul of guns in Swad.

16/1/61   Two bombs discovered in a haystack near Mullan Customs post.

29/1/61   Mullan bridge and a wide area of road surface was badly damaged by an explosion. This greatly disrupted private and public transport.

11/4/61   Mullan hut blown up for the fourth time since 1956.

4/8/61   Two men carrying guns and ammunition were arrested on the Swanlinbar/Ballinamore road.

28/8/61   Timber bridge at Caldragh, Kinawley blown up.

5/9/61   R.U.C. officers fired at a party of men attempting to cross the border at Gortoral.

Memorial to Patrick Mc Manus in Killaghaduff cemetery

As young adolescents with a rather romanticized concept of the I.R.A., its arms raids and ambushes, we didn't immediately recognize the terrible tragedy that was the death of other Irishmen like 23 year old RUC Constable Sean Scally, killed during the second raid on Derrylin barracks or the terrible outrage that took place on January 27 when off-duty Constable Norman Anderson (26) was treacherously gunned to death by an I.R.A. party after saying goodnight to his girlfriend. This was publicly condemned by Sean Lemass, Cardinal Conway and Dr. O' Callaghan, Bishop of Clogher and was to be one of the final nails in the 'Harvest' coffin.

By the time the I.R.A. Army Council publicly announced the ending of the campaign on February 26, 1962, most of us had come to realize that the whole campaign had been an unqualified failure, that it drove a wedge still further between the Unionist and Nationalist communities thus dealing a real hammer blow to any prospect of unity in the near future. 12 IRA men had been killed and many others had been injured. 6 RUC men also lost their lives and a further 32 were wounded.

The IRA eventually split into two factions – the Official IRA and the Provisional IRA. The Provisionals remained involved in what came to be known as 'The Troubles' from 1969 to 1997. If the deaths and injuries sustained during 'Operation Harvest' failed to highlight the folly of war, what followed during this period - the terrible atrocities and mass murders in places like Omagh and neighbouring Enniskillen, the British army massacre of unarmed civilians in Derry on 'Bloody Sunday' 1972, the bombing of the Abercorn restaurant in '72 and Patsy Mc Gurk's Bar in '73, the Miami massacre in 1975, the fate of 'the disappeared', the senseless killings of innocents such as Jonathan Ball aged 3, twelve year old Tim Perry, 15 year old Geraldine O' Reilly and 16 year old Patrick Stanley and so on - would leave the vast majority unequivocally opposed to armed combat as a means of sorting out our problems. When someone was killed or injured, we were no longer concerned whether the 'he' or the 'she' was or wasn't 'one of ours'.

At a personal level, two incidents in particular drove home the point. Sergeant Peter Gilgunn, aged 26, a native of Belcoo and a very friendly fellow boarder in St. Patrick's College, Cavan, was shot dead during a gun attack on his R.U.C. patrol car in the Creggan Road, Derry on January 27, 1972. He joined the force in 1966 shortly after leaving college and was promoted four years later. He was married and had an 8 month old son. Peter and his 20 year old Protestant colleague, David Montgomery, who was due to get married the following June, were the first policemen to be killed in the city during 'The Troubles'. Seven years later on 19th May 1979, Jack Mc Clenaghan (ex U.D.R.) aged 64, a married man with two children from nearby Edenmore, Florencecourt, who often had his lunch in my aunt's restaurant in Tullyhammon, was shot dead while delivering bread in Garrison, Co. Fermanagh. Jack used to give me a lift to Enniskillen when I was returning from holidays in my grandmother's house. I will always remember him as as a decent, jolly man, who chatted and joked and enjoyed talking about his family holidays in Killarney and elsewhere as we cruised along in his bread-van from Tullyhammon to Enniskillen away back in the '50's. Peter's and Jack's deaths made me particularly conscious of the fact that when you can put a face on a victim of warfare, it radically alters your perspective. At the end of the day, Peter, a Catholic and Jack, a Protestant,

A 'relic of oul dacency' -the remains of the last Mullan Customs Post

just wanted to earn a bob and get on with the business of living. Their deaths, like those of the 3701 others killed during 'The Troubles' must have brought unimaginable anguish to their loved ones. Our world was diminished by their untimely deaths.

'Operation Harvest' and 'The Troubles' seem a long way off now. Much has happened since and hopefully, many lessons have been learnt. Now that Sinn Fein and the D.U.P. have formed a new power-sharing executive, we can dare to hope, like 'Big Ian', that 'old suspicions and discord may be buried under the prospect of mutual and respectful co-operation'.

> *'The time for healing of the wounds has come,*
> *The moment to bridge the chasms that divide us has come*
> *The time to build is upon us ...'* Nelson Mandela

Garda Kyne and Garda Murtagh with Jim Casey *(Customs officer)* and Mary Mc Govern
at the Eire frontier barrier. Ben Aughlin in the background.
Photo Mary Gallagher (nee McGovern)

Anything to Declare?

Will he come out? Not in this rain, he won't!
Dismissively he waved us on. We rose from our saddles and pedalled hard,
Fearful that he might change his mind and raid our 'stash' of 'Golden Cow'!

A large brown galvanized shed, formerly a local dance hall, situated on the northern side of the village, came to be known as 'The Customs Hut'. From here officers tried to ensure that no prohibited goods or vehicles illegally entered the 'Free State'. The main idea was to protect home-produced items from foreign competition.

All drivers travelling to or from Northern Ireland had to get their 'pass' books stamped and their cars or lorries checked in or out at 'The Hut' before proceeding. Also, if you wished to cross the Border outside normal opening hours (8a.m. to 12 midnight), you had to 'put in a request', stating the time of your return and pay a fee that varied over the years from one and sixpence to five shilling. Failure to do so could leave you stranded at the border until the post re-opened next morning. Motorists from Northern Ireland, who wished to cross over and back had to renew their triptych (a kind of passport) each year and thus show that their vehicles had been 'bonded'. You had to pay duty on certain goods purchased in the North and if you didn't declare these or were caught taking them across roads, fields, rivers or lakes, you had to pay fines, run the risk of having your goods and vehicle impounded and in some extreme cases, face a term of imprisonment. Customs officials not only manned but also patrolled the unapproved roads.

When growing up, we had a very special relationship with the officers as we lived next door to their hut. Occasionally, they used to call on my father to come to their assistance whenever the odd rat would cross their boundary without 'a request'! He would set his cage and next day we'd see a 'poor ould divil' doing his nut inside.

On a brighter note, the men sometimes allowed us to stamp the books of passing motorists or challenged us to the odd game of 'Snap' or 'Rings' when things were slack. At Christmas time men like Bill Lynch, Tom Prunty and Mick Conway used to tell us about Santa passing the frontier post, how he enquired about our behaviour during the year and sought directions to our house. They also passed on privileged information about his reindeers (e.g. how Prancer needed a poultice to remove a thorn from his foot), about Santa's cargo and the general state of his health! Mick didn't mind if you kept an eye on him as he focused his 'Point Twenty-two' on a rabbit. That was before myxamatosis practically wiped out the bunnies in 1954.

Norbert Reilly, a colourful character from Ballyjamesduff, was only too pleased to get a pull whenever he set up his glider in a nearby field. The Pied Piper of Hamlin would not have had a 'look in' when the same excise officer, dressed as Santa and laden with presents, drove into town at Christmas in Patrick Lunney's old open-backed Dodge numbered 1L 1212. Swad people will remember many other men who served in the 'Customs' over the years – Pat Flynn, Peadar Cassidy, Joe Curran, John D. Cashin and his son Aiden, Noel Smith, Jim Woods, John Clare, Oliver Lynch, Al Harty, Finbarr Oakley and Frank Cafferty to name but a few.

Back row: Tom Prunty *(Customs officer)*, Johnny Prior and Mickey 'Bunnoe' O' Donoghue *(Bus drivers)* and Mick Conway *(Customs officer)*. Front row: Frank Mc Govern and Paddy Leydon *(Bus conductors)* with Paddy's son, Michael. Inset- Bill Lynch *(Customs officer)*.

The Northern officers operated from another frontier post just across the border at Mullan and were assisted by a patrol squad known locally as 'The Water Rats'. A genial official called Willie White manned that hut for years. The poor fellow had his office blown up more times by the I.R.A. than he cared to remember. Away back in 1938 my father was given a large parcel at the G.N.R. depot in Cavan to be left in the Northern hut for collection next day. It was addressed to a fictitious Mr. Wilson, Market Street, Enniskillen. Mr. George Hicks, from Florencecourt, who was acting as a Relief Customs Officer at the time, put the case under the heavy table in the office but that night at five minutes to eleven the time-bomb went off, wrecking the entire building. It had been raining earlier and a few men had taken shelter for some time in the doorway of the hut. Fortunately for them, they had headed off before the explosion. Afterwards, Willie joked that having a friend like my father, he didn't need an enemy!

People living close to the border mastered the art of outwitting the Customs men. Creamery cans, horse bags, hearses, coffins and apparel such as knickers and bras served to conceal illicit items! Some ladies crossed the border looking quite puny but displayed miraculous growth on their return just a few hours later! During the war years, one shabbily dressed fellow cycled past the Customs Post on such a regular basis that he aroused the suspicions of the officers but whenever they checked his bags, they never discovered any dutiable goods on board. However, it transpired that he was doing a nice steady country trade selling bicycles, bicycle tyres, tubes and accessories – contraband virtually unobtainable on this side at the time! Then there was the incident of the two Clones women returning from a northern expedition one very hot day in July. They were well endowed with contraband carefully stowed in every nook and cranny! Just after they crossed a hump-backed bridge, they espied a mobile customs unit ahead. 'We're done for now,' says one. 'Don't worry,' says the other, 'if you have the bread buttered, I have the tea wet!'

Butter, bacon and meat rationing was introduced in Northern Ireland in January 1940. Clothes rationing followed in 1941. Shops in the South held a plentiful supply of butter, eggs, meat, sugar, chocolate, cigarettes and tobacco, clothes and footwear and so there was a lot of trafficking in these items. Whiskey was also a 'big hit'. On the other hand, car batteries, electrical parts, tyres, razor blades, horse-shoe iron, horse-shoe nails, coal, flour and nylons were more readily available up North. These were regularly exchanged for our eggs, sugar, wines, spirits etc. In the 1950's there was a great run on Sulphate of Ammonia, a form of artificial manure. It was highly subsidised by the British government and so could be bought in the North for as little as ten shillings a bag. It was sometimes brought across mountainous terrain by donkey and creel and sold in the South for around £3 a bag. The R.U.C., as well as the Customs, kept a close watch for anyone trading in the stuff.

Smuggling cattle became big business from the early 1930's when the British government imposed tariffs on animals imported from the Free State. It got a further boost in the '40's and '50's when cattle prices rose dramatically in the north and calf subsidies (known as 'punch money') were introduced there. Once the Northern customs and police got their act together, smugglers had to resort to taking their animals across the border by fields, lakes and mountains, usually under cover of darkness. It was a hazardous occupation but helped many people to survive during the lean, hungry years. However, it did not always yield a good return. If caught, your animals were seized and you could end up in Crumlin Road jail.

The smuggling of pigs, especially suckers, was another profitable racket. It had one major drawback. The little buggers had a fierce propensity to squeal! Luckily, someone discovered that a drop of stout could send them into a deep sleep and this solved the problem.

As most of the 'Free State' Customs officers were either married locally, had girlfriends in the village or drank in the taverns there, prospective smugglers were often able to get some inkling of the travelling squad's time-table and work around it! Unfortunately, data on the rosters of their northern counterparts were more difficult to obtain.

A Customs officer's lot was not always a happy one. In 1940, for example, there was the infamous 'Battle of Dowra'. A large group of men were caught smuggling donkey loads of flour. This was 8 shillings a sack cheaper in Northern Ireland at the time. Several officers were injured in the ensuing struggle during the course of which most of the flour was destroyed. It was said that several of the Customs men took sick leave the next day and that a Garda Sergeant, who tried to restore some semblance of order, had to take to his bed for a full week. In the 'heel of the reel', 17 men were fined £100 each on smuggling charges at Dowra Court in

Mary Mc Govern with St.Mary's Hall under construction and old Customs 'hut' in background

Photo Mary Gallagher (nee McGovern)

THE FERMANAGH HERALD, SATURDAY, APRIL 25, 1958

Irish Customs Officers threatened

REMARKABLE evidence of how a number of Customs officers were threatened with iron bars while a lorry was lifted over a crater into the Six Counties at Aghafin, Clones, at 2.30 a.m. on October 3rd last, was related at Clones Court, before Justice P. Lavery, during the hearing of a Customs case.

A clipping from The Fermanagh Herald, April 25 1958 detailing the dangers of being a Customs Officer!

September that year. A somewhat similar confrontation occurred at Bragan, near Smithboro, Co. Monaghan, where one officer was reputed to have locked himself in his patrol car in order to protect himself from the wrath of the smugglers. The 'Blacklion News' in a 1943 copy of the 'Anglo Celt' reported that 'two married women from over the border were remanded to Dowra Court on £200 bail, charged with throwing a pot of paint at a Customs officer in Blacklion.' Occasionally officers had red faces for a different reason - when they discovered that cattle they had impounded 'escaped' under cover of darkness! The fact that roads and railway lines crossed and re-crossed the border, that some individual houses straddled it and that there wasn't a signpost in sight also gave them some terrible headaches.

The following list of items seized by a few Customs officers during the first three months of 1947 gives some idea of the variety of goods brought across the border at that time.

1 pair of men's boots	2 bottles of Sandeman's Port
20 gallons of lubricating oil	2 bicycles
2 bottles of whiskey	Paraffin oil
2 tons of sulphate of ammonia	8 bottles of gin
4 lb. of ham	3 donkeys
8 coffins	14,000 fishing hooks
Loaves of bread	64 ounce hanks of fishing line tobacco
Cigarettes	

The fact that 11,000 cases of smuggling were reported on the Irish land frontier in 1945 tells its own story.

In June 1941, horses and traps were seized on the border at Mullan by British Customs and the R.U.C. under the law prohibiting horses and vehicles from crossing over and back without proper documentation. This presented a real problem for those who liked to travel to Mass in Swad by trap. Fortunately, an amicable solution was eventually found. In April 1942, a Swanlinbar grocer was fined at Enniskillen Petty Sessions for dealing in prohibited goods including 5cwts. of coffee!

The price of goods North and South varied from time to time. Items brought one way were later smuggled in the opposite direction.

In the 1950's butter was much cheaper in the North and I usually got the job of picking it up at Mc Carron's of Kinawley; my pay, a packet of Spangles. Once the business was done, I would glide along with some Golden Cow firmly squeezed on the back carrier of my bike, the rest in shopping bags, dangling from the handlebars in front. By luck or good guidance, no customs patrol ever stopped me in my tracks. However, on one occasion just after I passed Stumpy Hall on the unapproved back road, I did spot a uniformed official in the distance and had to bide my time picking blackberries until the coast was clear!

Isn't it hard to believe you can now cross over and back without any fuss? 'The old order changeth yielding place to new'. That's the way!

Changing Times - Dr. Ian Paisley and Bertie Ahern at Oldbridge House, the site of the Battle of the Boyne (1690).
Photo courtesy of Colin Keegan (Photographer) and Collins Photo Agency.

COPING WITH CHANGE

The only constant in our world today is change

I'll conclude with this 'tribute' to anyone waiting in the 'Departure Lounge' or entering what our old friend Micheál O'Hehir might have referred to as 'injury time'! It was inspired by an anonymous contributor to a Google web-site.

We were born before colour television, CD's, videos or iPods. We lived before credit cards, laser beams, dishwashers, microwave ovens, tumble driers, electric blankets, air conditioners, drip dry clothes, car safety belts, multi-storey car parks, motorways, fish fingers, Kentucky Fried Chicken, smoothie makers, ballpoint pens, food processors, powerhoses and pantihose, bikinis and paninis, Bratz, Barney the stuffed dinosaur, Dora the Explorer, therapeutic MBT's (Masai Barefoot Technology), hair straighteners, digital cameras and plasma screens. Little did we think we'd ever take money from a hole in the wall or see a man walking on the moon?

We got married first and then lived together. Weren't we 'away with the fairies'! We thought fast food was what you ate during Lent. A 'Big Mac' was an oversized raincoat you were damn glad to take with you to a match in Clones or in Leonard's field. We knew more about body odour than body language. Back then our politicians could be seen at funerals rather than tribunals. Now they've gone airy-dairy - they milk the place dry and then develop 'Milk of Amnesia'!

We were born before crèches and disposable nappies, job-sharing and career breaks. We ate our dinner in the middle of the day. Twas a long way from bagels, French brie and sundried tomatoes we were rared.

For us a chip was a piece of wood or a fried potato, a web was something a spider made, people panicked when they saw a mouse and spam was a kind of tinned luncheon meat. Hardware meant nuts, bolts, metal tools and implements and 'software' hadn't been invented. As for a lap-top, the only lap we knew was our mother's, a circuit of Mac of the Lawn's field on Sports Day or the roundy fellow in the hay-field.

Before 1945 a stud was something that fastened a collar to your shirt, 'going all the way' meant staying on the bus till you got to Enniskillen or Cavan, and 'having it off' usually referred to a bandage or 'Plaster of Paris. The only pill we knew was an Aspro.

In our day, grass was mown, Coke was a cold drink or a solid fuel, a joint was a disreputable establishment or a piece of meat you had on a Sunday (if you were lucky), and pot was a deep, round container you used for cooking or kept under the bed for emergencies. Blocks of Calvita and Galtee triangles wrapped in foil were synonymous with cheese and wine was for the altar. Loaves were either batch or pan. There was none of your ciabatta, pitta or sourdough. You could have your tea strong or light. Noel was the only Coffey we knew. Rice was for dessert, Curry was a small village in County Sligo and Olive Oil was only available in chemist shops.

We were certainly not before the difference between male and female was discovered, but we were surely before the sex change and plastic surgery; we made do with the 'bits and pieces' we had. We were the last generation that was so dumb as to think you had to be married to have a baby, and we didn't really believe it could happen to a bishop.

Now we write everything down. We hide the front door key but can't remember where we left it. Our knees buckle but our belts won't. We've ingrown toe-nails and have outgrown sex. We're at least 17+ around the neck, 44 around the waist and 110 around the golf course. Our backs go out more often than we do. We stick our teeth in steaks and they lodge there. Most of us haven't seen our knees for years. If we do bend to tie our laces, or to pick up the fallen soap in the shower, we wonder what else we should be doing while we're down. We, who were born before the war ended in 1945, are indeed a hardy bunch when you think of the ways the world has changed and the adjustments we have had to make. It's no wonder we get a little confused at times. No matter, we're still here or thereabouts. Shure isn't that the way!